— BLUE MARBLE REVIEW —

blue
marble
review

five-year anthology

edited by molly hill

ISBN 13: 978-1-63489-399-2
Library of Congress Catalog Number has been applied for.
Printed in the United States of America
First Printing: 2021

25 24 23 22 21   5 4 3 2 1

Cover design by Jack Walgamuth
Interior design by Patrick Maloney

Wise Ink Creative Publishing
807 Broadway St NE
Suite 46
Minneapolis, MN, 55413

The first issue of *Blue Marble Review* was published in March of 2016, and this anthology represents a selection of work from the past twenty-four online published issues. This book is dedicated to student readers, writers, and artists all over the world.

"And by the way, everything in life is writable about if you have the outgoing guts to do it, and the imagination to improvise. The worst enemy to creativity is self-doubt."

—Sylvia Plath

contents

featured art

introduction

Blue Marble Review began five years ago as an online writing experiment inspired by the first line in a Mary Oliver poem, "The Buddha's Last Instruction":

Make of yourself a light.

Our aim was to be a story collective, not only a place where students could send writing, get published, and be paid for their work but also an online site that would connect writers and readers. We believed students could feel a sense of shared humanity through experiencing the creativity of other student writers. We hoped that a broad collection of stories, poems, essays, and art from different cultures and life experiences might prove to be illuminating.

We've been lucky—five years of online publishing, scores of submissions and readers, and now our first print anthology.

To date we've published close to 600 students, from just over three dozen countries. With those numbers we knew we couldn't make a *best of* anthology; there was just too much good writing and art to choose from. So, we're going with our *first of*—an anthology of selected work from our first five years and what we hope will be the first of many print collections.

Blue Marble Review is staffed by a rotating group of dedicated editors who read, review, and rate poetry, fiction, and nonfiction submissions as part of the selection process for each issue. To current masthead staff, Arushi Avachat, Aditi Desai, Meili Gong, Isabella Milacnik, Kate Schiltz, Priscilla Trinh, and Alexa Vos: thank you. We're so fortunate to team up with editors who are dependable, succinct, talented—and on deadline.

We're sincerely grateful to all who have read, written, edited, donated to, emailed, and supported *Blue Marble Review* during our five years of online publication. To the many wonderful student writers worldwide who've discovered us through a teacher, mentor, friend, writing center, or search engine: keep writing and creating! Thank you for writing about hopes and hard things, dreams that came true and fell flat, as well as sharing a bit about where you're headed and the places you've been along the way.

This book would not have been possible without the diligence, inspiration, and hard work of student editors Priscilla Trinh, Alexa Vos, and Kate Schiltz, one-time Tonka Writers turned college achievers, who were invaluable in the selection process for this anthology. If there were a gold medal for careful attention to reviewing each submission in every issue of our archives—these three would share the top of the podium.

And finally, this anthology is dedicated to every student who took the time to write and submit poetry, stories, rants, essays, photos, and artwork, whether you were published or not. We're grateful for your interest in our journal and for trusting us with your insightful, sad, funny, quirky, serious, sophisticated, but always illuminating creative work. What a privilege it is to provide a platform to showcase the work of so many young people on the way up.

at the cedar lee theater

Annie Ertle

How important and how conscious and how *good* we feel
When we crowd into the small independent theater and we settle next
To groups of diverse strangers in head scarves with NPR tote bags
And we watch the documentary that details
The horror of Women That Are Not Us.

We gasp and we cluck at the appropriate moments.
We "thank God that doesn't happen here"
And we wonder what we can do to help
In between fistfuls of popcorn that leave our hands greasy,
Our tongues thirsting for the Diet Coke they paraded around in the ads.

We fantasize about fundraisers and we hashtag the tweets and for
The next twenty-four hours we lie in bed staring at the ceiling,
Prophesizing about what would have happened if that had been us,
Not them, and we feel guilty until the weight of our down comforters
Hugs us to sleep and we are calm and we are safe and we are okay.

Then the details of our lives overtake us and oh god the grocery
List is so long and the laundry piles up and the assignments are
Coming due and the house is a mess and when did life get so hard?

I remember there are two types of people in this world, and I'm lucky
Because I get to be the spectator and not the subject,
The person who pays the $10.50 admission, a temporary redemption.

The women documented in the movie stood up to the Taliban
And I was too afraid to ask the people sitting beside me in the neat row
If they could just scoot so I could slip by and get a head start
On living this normal life that I, for whatever reason, have won.

The advertising posters begin to peel and are torn down until
Next week, when new movies are released and new injustices recounted.

october

Anthony DiCarlo

The setting sun beckons all fiery things toward their rest
As autumn leaves fall like embers toward the dark earth.
I walk home across cinders,
And each step replies with crackling sparks.

thoughtknot

Anishi Patel

time is a treasure — so that must mean it's another man's trash — or perhaps a woman — i don't know anything — or anyone — so many walls in my imagination — but not like a maze, no, more like boxes upon boxes that transcend the metaphorical box — but have you ever wondered why it's a box? — because i like triangles and circles and irony — a box within the capital B box — and the walls, four walls, round walls, holed walls that are all walls — because if you think too long, anything — is a wall — and now my tea has spilled, and it burns — but that's flavored water under the bridge that flows like supply and demand — over the bumps in my wallflower hand — and why save the baby clothes — memory is sad — tomorrow i'm out of my mind but today it's all in my head — these endings, they come in boxes, and boxes packed so tightly with goodbyes are inseparable — so isn't it better to forget, says the thinkmuscle, that slave to sleep and time, but never to rhyme — and now i've spilled my milk and it's creamy and cream is frothy and froth is light — in relation to what? — i don't understand relativity, but that's beside my point — not that i would know what's beside or behind or on top of my point because i seem to have lost it — which means i'm in the black cat's path — so i wonder is that good luck, bad luck, or perhaps i never knew of superstition in which case it is bliss — obviously, it doesn't matter because i gave the cat a fish and it came to the bridge under which i spilled my tea and relative milk and here — there's many fish, so the cat does not leave — why? because I did not teach it to fish.

garlic toast

Sierra Woelfel

You left me out
To get hard and stale
And now
I'm just crusty
You might as well bake me
Into garlic bread
So someone will appreciate me
That someone
Won't be you
I know

I know that you don't like it
You hate garlic
And that's why
I want to cover myself in it
And make myself into
The best damn garlic bread
I can possibly be
Because I don't need you
To be me

narrow roads

Alexa Bocek

Our conversations have narrowed
What were once wide
And busy highways
Are now dirt country
Backroads, almost
Bike paths or walking trails
They are slender streets with
Unlit lampposts
We've been reduced to talk of
Cigarette prices and
"How's your mother been?"
"Good, thanks for asking"
Sometimes I catch you on roads
We've been down before
You've asked me questions
Three or four times since
I met you and the answer hasn't
Changed. Our lanes are lacking
Soon I suppose
We will meet a dead end
But when I think of how
Our spacious streets were once
Open and endless, like we'd
Be driving forever,
I cannot stop the car

we do not apologize now

Jordan Ferdman

We are in tenth grade, and she cannot be older than thirty. She is new to our school as we are new to womanhood, and when boys in class cut us off, she does not even glance their way. Her eyes remain fixed on us, even as our voices dwindle, and she doesn't tear her gaze away until we finish our thoughts with a period. When our voices dance into octaves, concluding our thoughts with question marks or apologies, she lifts a manicured eyebrow and shakes her head to coax us onwards to a resounding conclusion.

Her personal life is infinitely interesting to us. She does not wear a ring, but we think she is too pretty to not be married. We also know she would find deep flaws in that line of thinking, but we can't bring ourselves to care too much; outside her class, we learn quickly that pretty is the best thing we could hope to be. We wonder if, when she looks in the mirror, she is happy with what she sees. We wonder if the men in her life treat her well. We wonder how she comforts her friends when the men in their lives don't treat them well. We wonder if she thinks about us when we are not at school. She assigns exuberant amounts of weekend homework, and though we never discuss it, we think that is deliberate. We think and hope that she wants us safe in our rooms on a Saturday night, kneeling over a textbook instead of some boy.

She assigns more homework than any other teacher, and though we text each other nightly complaints—how much time does she think we have to spend on her class?—assignments are always finished in cherubic yearnings of "good job!" scribbled across the top in red ink. We exist in a constant state of anticipating praise, of batting our eyes and shrugging down our shirts and hoping to be good enough. In her class, praise does not come with soreness and pain. In her class, we do not ice our throbbing knees with praise but paste it in our notebooks as a reminder that she cares.

The boys in our class do not like her much. They say that she is a bitch, and though we can't quite articulate it, we know that they cannot think of any other words to insult her. Once, when she raised her arm to write on the whiteboard, she revealed a small stain of dampness under her arm and the boys snickered. She did not notice, or if she did, she didn't react, and we stared at her, wondering how she was able to be so unabashedly human.

She does not say anything when one of us leaves the classroom with crinkling plastic up our sleeve or comes in ten minutes late with red-rimmed eyes. She does not hide her horror when we recount what the old math teacher whispered as we left the room. She does not apologize for cursing, does not apologize for anything.

Imagine Jennifer . . . we start our sentences, draped over each other in the library or on the bus. The latter half usually involves something sexual or banal—as we learned quickly, some things were both—and it is unclear which is more exciting. Does she have three emergency Midol, two tampons, and a Hershey's Kiss tucked in the front pocket of her bag? Does she refuse to go down on boyish men, ask them why they want her mouth for their pleasure and not her words?

We wonder what she was like in tenth grade. We wonder if she looked down at her thighs and wanted to disappear, if she cried while getting her bikini line waxed, if she drank too much and did homework on Sunday with a hangover. We wonder if she was always the way she is now, and deep down, we hope not. We hope she found it somewhere, and we hope that it's out there for us too.

how we talk about juliet

Amanda Lee

i.

Botanically: as the blushing rose named
for her, vivisected into light-shy
            petals.   On the flower
-laced continuum of taxonomy
we scatter her somewhere between
inanimate object and heroine.

ii.

Linguistically: we assign her the word
"devoted" and move on to Romeo.
But shouldn't we stop and debate if she, too,
can be strong? Debate if women can be
            workers
                        breadwinners?
Only two women debate in Parliament.

iii.

Mathematically: equate her relationships. Love
is the product of physical beauty. Is this
why my friends starve themselves?
            Strawberry juice
is the colour of botched
skin after plastic surgery, blood
seeping through botoxed smiles.

iv.

Artistically: paint her pale-skinned, baby-
curled, trailing damask. We hand her
         a button
for modesty. Then criticize her
for her short skirts, hot pink
binders and crop tops.

v.

Astronomically: hold our hands against the same
         constellations   Juliet
looked up to when Romeo left her   lost
and alone. We watch the moon wax and
wane, looking for a line of best fit
through this
star-crossed path.

waterloo teeth

Ellora Sutton

My canine is my great-great-grandmother's.
Yellowed with age,
a well-read page.
The sediment
is fossilised with fables.
When I am lost,
I trace it with my tongue-tip
and soak up the Braille.

The burial mound of my wisdom tooth
is my ancestral aunt's,
sleeping snug
like the lump of Australian opal
she left me.
A treasure, a milky thing.
A stone breast
resting in the gum
of the scarlet cloak
we keep in the airing cupboard.

My sunflower seed bucktooth
is from the farm girl
that would germinate into
some flying bird part of me.
It is strong and broad

and the first thing you see,
a placard:
This girl is of the earth.

My third incisor is Victorian.
It tastes of elderflower cordial
and sepia photographs,
and reminds me
that even when I stand still,
stay silent,
time blurs past.

The altar of my molar,
nobody knows who that came from.
I think it is soft enough
to have been swept up
from the ashes
of witch-fire.
I can taste the scream of it,
and maybe that's why
my lips have such a temper.

becoming nancy

Yuwei Dou

At age thirteen, I lived on the fifth floor of Ya Qing Court, a gray apartment building with many windows that overlooked the street. There, we called the smog over the city the yellow dragon because it made the sky perpetually yellow, and people often wore masks outside. A few Yang trees sat across the Beijing street in a courtyard. On the ground floors of apartment buildings were shops where vendors from the country sold candied fruit called tanghulu and guokui pork pancake. Multicolored awnings always flapped in the wind, and old men sat in their rickshaws waiting to carry passengers to their destinations. Down the street, my school was a complex of sterile white buildings that resembled a jail. Whenever I left the streets and entered the gates of No. 241 middle school, I felt as if I were leaving freedom and entering a courthouse where a strict jury would judge me.

In that school, our teachers were our guides, judges, prosecutors, and executioners. They wielded immense power. One winter, I made Ms. Liu's face turn red when I privately corrected her use of future tense in English. She sent me outside without a coat, and I stood there for twelve hours shivering in the snow. Often children stood with me who were also sent outside to stand in the snow. Sometimes I could see a hundred children, standing in a line outside, shivering, contemplating their mistakes.

In school, I knew a girl named Nancy. She was the kind of girl who would not eat her hot pot and dumplings outside like the other women while the men ate inside, as was common in Chinese culture. She insisted on eating at the table with the men. She loved hip-hop dancing and ping-pong. While the rest of us left our hair black, Nancy dyed her hair golden. Her legs were pale and long. Nancy always smelled like laundry detergent, as if her clothes were cleaner than ours. Unlike most of us, she was an Opera God: kind and good and gave everyone luck. Each day, she would encourage her friends: Keep working hard! Have a good day! We lived in a bamboo-steamer-like environment, where every kind word was a cure for death.

Naturally, she didn't belong in this place. Nancy was like the tiger locked in the zoo. While the rest of us understood our cages, Nancy seemed to quietly pace crazily. We all should have noticed when she began to change.

One day, she stopped smiling. When the teacher called on her, she stood up and said nothing. I thought she was having her period, but then I was too worried about my own problems to help.

On a Wednesday when we arrived at the school, news that Nancy was missing spread quickly on campus. That day, the rain and clouds converged to form a gray dragon in the sky. The whole day, teachers didn't seem to notice her absence. Even our counselor ate her sandwich in her office and watched television operas. But we students secretly thought Nancy had run away to another city, like Holden in *The Catcher in the Rye,* and would be back. But Nancy's tall, lean figure remained noticeably absent.

Two days later, I read about her in the city newspaper. They didn't mention Nancy's name to protect her identity, but we all knew.

Rumors spread that Nancy was staying in a shabby motel. I knew the place. From traffic and pollution, the outside wall of the motel long ago turned from white to dirty yellow and was covered with patches of small ads. From her boyfriend, I found out that Nancy was smoking marijuana, playing games on her phone, and eating the 3-for-$1 mysterious-meat pancakes sold on the street.

While riding the bus one day to the library, I passed the motel and saw Nancy wearing our school's uniform, but it was oil stained. Her pants looked wet, as if she'd washed them but didn't have a dryer. Without shoes on, she was standing at the door of her motel room. She gazed straight ahead, and her normally happy eyes looked as if they held a secret. Her long hair looked like that of a homeless woman. For weeks, she stayed there in that terrible motel, skipping school, smoking marijuana, and setting a bad example for all of us. She was my hero. When our teachers weren't around, some of us said quietly to each other, "I want to be Nancy, even for one day. One hour. So I can stop studying for just a little while." When we said those words, our faces looked like those of mischievous, scared children. Secretly, we spoke about the joy of playing soccer on a field under the pleasant sunshine or riding the Cinderella's Secret Palace at Disneyland in Shanghai.

But our words changed when teachers' pets interjected: "Nancy was such a bad girl. Ms. Lee cannot get the extra prize this month for being a good teacher. We will never be like Nancy!" But secretly, we were all Nancy. We all felt that hidden desire to throw away our futures to go lie in some dingy motel, where life was devoid of pressure, where mysterious meat pancakes were better than egg tarts from Crazy Bakery and unending school. To us, that terrible, frightening life was better than the one we lived every day.

The situation changed when the principal cornered Nancy's boyfriend and threatened to beat him if he didn't tell her where Nancy was hiding out. Pretty soon, the police were dragging Nancy into the principal's office. I remember watching the armed officers escort her across the blacktop to the office. Like a criminal, she looked at her feet the whole time. Her face looked sick, weak, dirty, and wild. I could see a tear in her shirt and her pants, as if she'd run through trees to escape judgment, as if she had been willing to risk harm rather than return.

Later I heard that the principal beat Nancy with her bare hands, screaming, "You've hurt our reputation! Now the education government is punishing us by taking money from our school!" When Nancy arrived home, her dad beat her so angrily that he injured her leg. Beatings were normal in China. Parents and teachers beat their children as a way of teaching them life experience. Later that week, at her apartment, Nancy stood on the ledge of the window, but her parents stopped her. She tried to grab a knife, but her parents took her to the hospital, where she lived in a small, dark, windowless room for seven days, like an animal in a cage.

I never saw Nancy again and she never returned to school, but we still talk about her. She lives on in my mind, and I'm sure she lives on in the minds of other students who want freedom. Sometimes when I study biology for twenty hours straight and I feel evil in my brain, I throw my book across the room. I turn on my music, and for ten minutes I become Nancy. I become her.

the nothing of mark turner

Sylvia Nica

Nothing means flat kisses or abandoned shoe stores wrapping old memories around their legs like faded scarves. Nothing means the absence of words, an empty cola bottle, a lack of soul. A black hole is better than nothing. Emptiness is better than nothing.

The cold cola bottle clutched in my arms sweats fat droplets while the sidewalk paints my feet red. I contemplate the idea of flatness beneath the artificial blue sky. I heard the Earth was flat from the reedy boy in the desk in front of me. He argued with our physics teacher about trajectory and speed, screaming "Yes, but it's *Aristotle*..." I wasn't paying attention. I only noticed when his desk remained empty, when he became a stone fingernail in the yard.

Maybe the Earth is flat. The sky is flat, listless, to me. I wield my cola bottle and tear wisps from the sky, stuffing the blue cotton candy against my hot, dry gums. The sky tastes like water. The sky tastes like nothing. The sidewalk is so hot it fries my feet into bacon. I would say an egg, but that's a cliché, and clichés are husks. I am more original than the reedy boy in the Flat Earth Society. He vomited words others had digested, and then execrated, for thousands of years. I guess it killed him. Aristotle would shake his head, because if you say something long enough then it dies. People start thinking you're cracked as a metaphorical egg.

I am so cracked that my soul has evaporated through the breaks in my skin and formed a puddle of yolk on the sidewalk. That is why I feel useless. I am the abandoned shoe store distorted through my cola bottle, old memories threading my legs together until I cannot run. I take a swig of soda, feeling my yolk fry around my feet. I watch my name around the cola glass obscure the floating green buildings: MARK. So ordinary it is printed on a cola bottle. Maybe that is why I feel like I am splintered, because if you make something ordinary, it perishes. I am nice and ordinary.

I am a flat kiss, a missing shoe, a vacant hotel. My soul is a well-done omelet, no spices, my name so common it graces thousands of labels. A cracked-up loony, that's what I am, the ones you find dropped like pennies on street corners. I'll die alone in an alley, become a stone fingernail in a yard with trillions of hands. Maybe I'll join the reedy boy in Flat Heaven. We'll discuss Aristotle.

Do the laws of nature permit a yolk to be un-fried? The sidewalk is cold beneath my feet. The cola bottle, half empty, has stopped sweating in the sun. I take my last chug and look at the dusty buildings wavering through the green glass until they break into streaks of dirt. At least those Flat Earth guys have a purpose. I am drained like a bottle. I will flit around this dusty, abandoned town, grow old on cold cola and stray bits of cloud. It's not terrible to have an absence of purpose. When you die, your shell floats away, turns into sand. Your soul becomes

generation gap

Jaden Goldfain

My father repeats his question.

"If I told you I wanted to be a woman," he says, his words pressing into me like his fingers pressed around the kitchen counter edge, "what would you say?"

I know what he's doing. His question is hypothetical. He is Before me, challenging me to stay in his time. He wants me to stay where people have definitions. Standing After me is Their time (Our time?), where definitions are decimated. No ashes remain.

I pick up a blade and slash twice. Once through Before and once through After. I toss the weapon aside.

"Okay," I tell him. "I would say okay. I would not fight you."

He scoffs. I throw him a rope from where I stand, valleys on either side. "I would love you."

He doesn't catch it. The valley grows wider.

my girl lights fires

Avra Margariti

Bella slips into my bed reeking of smoke. She lays her palm against my cheek, and the oily residue it leaves behind makes me think of gasoline.

"What time is it?" I mumble into my pillow.

I try to roll over and face her, but she nudges me back and slings an arm around my waist.

This isn't the first time Bella has swung by after hours. Usually, her visits are accompanied by a fifth of vodka swiped from her family's liquor cabinet and a batch of kisses, delivered silently and breathlessly so as not to alert my mother sleeping down the hall.

She nuzzles my neck. "Don't worry about it. Go back to sleep."

I blame my next words on my dazed, surreal state of neither dream nor waking. "Did you miss me?"

Bella's laughter rolls like thunder and lightning through my body. "Very much."

When I wake up again Bella has gone, the sooty outline on my white sheets the sole proof she was ever here.

The next morning, my entire class is abuzz, an aberration from the expected lethargy of early-morning homeroom. My friend Markus leans against my desk.

"Hey, Laura. Did you hear about the fire in the old warehouse down Starfall Lane?"

"What?" I sputter, suddenly parched.

Markus nods. His crooked bangs swish back and forth with the force of his enthusiasm. "The entire west wing burned to a crisp last night. We used to play Spin the Bottle there. Crazy, right?"

"Crazy . . ." I bring the end of my braid to my nose. My hair still carries a faint fireside whiff. I remember with a jolt that it's Bella's and my one-month anniversary tomorrow.

Although we have different class schedules, Bella always manages to steal a pocket of time for me. My feet propel me through the hordes of students toward her locker. Faraway flames hiss in my ears.

"Where were you last night?" I blurt the moment I reach her, forgetting to be casual.

"In your room, being your own personal dream catcher," Bella replies.

Her warm chestnut eyes glimmer as her red-painted lips stretch into an easy smile; the picture of innocence. She leans in to kiss me, but I place a finger on her mouth to stop her approach. Her lip piercing brushes against my skin and sends a sizzling current coursing through me.

"Anyway," I say, trying to mask my labored breathing behind faux-indignation, "don't you have a class to get to? I'm not tutoring you if you fail."

Bella's unapologetic laughter rises above the bustle of the hallway. She opens her locker to retrieve her textbooks, and I peek inside. A picture of us, taken on an amusement-park date a week after she asked me out. The strawberry-colored teddy bear I won for her that same day. And pressed up against the bear, books of matches stacked in haphazard rows and a set of ash-stained clothes. I look away.

This is all so new, so fragile. I don't want Bella's secret to complicate things between us.

I don't wait for her after school. Instead, I trek past the gentrified part of town, to the old dirt roads running along the waterfront. I pause when I reach the abandoned warehouse, a pigeon-gray smear against the blue of the sky. Tilting my head back, I take in the entire dilapidated glory of it.

The first thing I notice when I squeeze through the gap in the chain-locked gate is the blanket of ash underfoot. It must have rained down from the cracks in the ceiling. It sticks in a thin film on my white sneakers and stains each fingerprint when I try to wipe it away. The big stairway leading to the upper floors is intact, and so are most of the rooms.

Markus might have been exaggerating, but it still looks bad. The west wing is torched, every wall kissed by the flames. The fire's memory lingers in the blackened charcoal spots and the scorched detritus accumulated on the floor. A smell of burnt hair permeates the air like a faulty hairdryer.

I imagine Bella standing in the doorway just as I am, the flames casting shadow and light across her face, her silver lip ring glittering like a fire-forged gem. Goosebumps bloom across my skin, and I don't know if it's due to unease or awe.

"So," Bella says, "how should we celebrate? I'm told one month is a milestone. Most high school relationships don't last past it. I don't know what the statistics for same-sex romance are, but you get the gist."

Her voice is nonchalant, but her eyes dart around the hallway without landing on anything and the toe of her shoe scuffs against the scarred linoleum floor.

All week, I had giddily filled page after page of my planner, trying to come up with the perfect anniversary date. Something classic, like dinner and an indie movie, or maybe something daring, like a romantic picnic where the entire town could see us. Instead, I find myself saying, "I've got too much homework. Plus, Mr. Ramirez hinted at a pop quiz tomorrow."

I tell myself that I'm putting the date off because of smoke and suspicions. But a little panicking part of me has wanted to pull the fire alarm on our relationship even before I visited the warehouse on Starfall Lane.

"Oh." Bella frowns for a moment before she paints a bright expression back across her face. "I could help you study. I know you're a nervous wreck right before a quiz."

"Sorry," I mumble. "I really need to ace this test."

"Don't worry about it," Bella says, her smile reassuring. "I'll find some other way to entertain myself."

I let her walk me to my next class with a searing certainty that I will be following her tonight.

Groggy, jittery, exhausted, I look for Bella first thing in the morning.

"I know what you did last night. I followed you." I want it to sound like an accusation, but my words are tired, losing steam.

Bella shoots me a smile, gone before I can decode it. "You think I didn't know? You're not as sneaky as you think."

I think of last night, the dumpster fires Bella left like a trail of bread crumbs across town.

"Why are you doing this? Don't you know it's dangerous? Not to mention illegal."

"I love watching the flames. They're beautiful, and they make my heart quiet."

I stare at her, unable to process her words. I expected her to deny it, or at least weave some lie. Not this crippling honesty. Her smile contains the duality of a child making mischief and a girl being humbled by a force of nature. It makes my throat tight with anger. With *longing*.

"I only burn things people don't need, and I'm always careful not to lose control of the fire. There are no witnesses. It's only me and . . ."

"Your messed-up hobby?" I snap. I can feel the cracks forming between us, a hairline fissure growing bigger, and I'm not sure if it's her doing or mine.

Bella's smile turns small and hurt before fading altogether. "Laura, come on. Talk to me. What is this really about?"

I take a step back when she reaches out to link our fingers together. For the first time since I met her, I evade her touch.

My breath rasps in and out of my throat; my tongue tastes like ash and charred meat. I don't even know why I'm so angry. It's because of the fires and the secrecy, sure. But as I stand there staring at her open expression, I realize something else. Maybe I'm looking for a reason to fight because I don't know if our relationship can withstand it.

The truth is, I've been having doubts about us. They creep up when Bella is away, and I start wondering why she would ever go out with me when she could have any boy or girl she wanted. They spike when boys I've known all my life ask if they can get a ticket to the "lesbian show." They cut deep when I watch the news, read the statistics, or when I hear the whispers in the hallways. And now, all of those worries are threatening to engulf us and the anniversary date I keep postponing.

"I . . . I have to go," I say, moving farther down the hallway, away from Bella and all the confusion caused by her presence.

She doesn't try to stop me but instead calls after me, "I'll be at the shipyard tonight. Please come."

Her dark eyes follow my retreat. I can feel their concern, their tenderness. The sensation of her gaze lingers even after I've burst out into the parking lot.

The truth is, I'm scared of the connection between us, those tight wires that quiver and pulse with electricity. I've never felt anything close to this before, and I don't know if I should embrace it or run away.

I'm afraid of getting burned, and it has nothing to do with matches or tinder.

Deep into the night, I lie in bed, thinking. I bury my nose in my pillow, but I only catch the scent of lavender detergent and my everyday shampoo. There's no trace of smoke. No proof that Bella was ever here. I get up and pace around the small space. My room is catalogue-perfect, everything in order—just as I like it. The only thing out of place is inside my drawer, tucked beneath my diaries and old school notebooks. I take out the box of matches I swiped from Bella's locker and twirl it between my fingers for a few minutes. A package so small. So harmless. So full of chaos and possibility.

I take the matches with me back to bed. At times I feel like my whole life is scripted, but this is new and unfamiliar. I want it to fill me with excitement, but my brain knows all too well how to be scared. So I bring Bella's face to mind. I imagine the way my pulse gets out of sync whenever she's near, another diversion from its steady, boring routine. Holding the matchbox makes me feel closer to her, somehow, and I don't shy away from the feeling.

Somewhere from within, I draw the courage to light the first match. I watch the tiny dancing flame, transfixed by the way it consumes the match's stick body. I don't notice when the flame reaches my thumb and forefinger. My fingers get singed, and I drop the dead match on my bed sheets. I imagine Bella beside me, taking my hand in hers ever so gently, teasing me a bit before she kisses it all better.

Lurching to my feet, I put on my coat in one swift motion. I don't feel scared walking the empty streets alone at night. I know Bella will be waiting for me, and that certainty is enough to light up the world.

The old shipyard has been out of use for decades. These days, it's an ancient, corroded husk whole generations of kids have been utilizing to ride their bikes and smoke their weed in secret. I've never done either of those things, but the thought of breaking the rules makes me feel like liquid fire is flowing through my bloodstream. Even before I've woven my way through the labyrinth of metal and decay, I catch the tell-tale gleam of flames.

Bella stands before a small open fire. Her hair is draped over one shoulder, a red scarf coiled twice around her neck.

"You came."

She doesn't disguise the relief in her voice. She keeps surprising me, this girl. We've been friends for almost a year and girlfriends for longer than a month, but I still don't know her all that well.

I *want* to know her, pyromania and all.

"This wasn't exactly the anniversary date I had in mind," I say.

I join her at the fire. For a few moments, we stand side by side, watching the flames flicker and tremble in their pit.

"Help me find more kindling?" Bella asks.

The fire illuminates her profile. Her eyelashes cast elongated shadows against the honey tint of the flames against her skin. It's beautiful. The fire. Her smile. Everything.

My breath catches in my throat.

I say, "Will you show me how to make the fire stronger?"

Her smile turns brilliant. I follow her around the shipyard. Together we gather dry branches and bunched-up newspapers to bring back to the cinderblock pit.

Bit by bit, I feed the fire, making it bigger, stronger. I watch the flames climb up to the night sky, blazing orange against pure black. I close my eyes, and the flames paint the back of my lids strawberry red. The crackling sounds combine with the smoky smell to touch a place inside me, somewhere close to my heart. I don't know what it is that makes Bella's heart so loud and unruly that only starting fires can soothe it, but her presence has always quieted the maddening whir of my brain.

I reach out blindly and grasp Bella's hand in mine. Our fingers interlace, and I feel more right than I've felt in a long time.

"I'm sorry I've been so afraid," I say, trusting that Bella will know I'm not referring to the fires.

"It's not your fault," she says gently. "I know you came out of the closet because of me. Maybe you weren't ready. But you should know I'm here for you, even if you don't want us to be together anymore."

My eyes fly open. "No. I want you."

I didn't come out to the world because of Bella; I did it *for* her. For us. I wanted to be the kind of girlfriend she deserved, not someone trapped, ashamed, and afraid of her own shadow. And maybe I failed at that last part, but not anymore.

Bella smiles, fire and stars and determination in her brown eyes. "And I want you too."

I'm the one who initiates the kiss. It's sweet like a sugared fruit at first. Slow, maybe a bit tentative. I pour all the love and frustration of this last month into it, all the uncharted hope I discovered within myself tonight. Then her piercing rubs against the inside of my lips and sends sizzling sparks of electricity from my tingling mouth all the way to my toes.

When our mouths part, Bella laughs and pulls me into a hug. Entwined, we stand before the fire. I close my eyes again and allow the warmth to envelop me.

letters

Stephen Duncanson

Everyone at the bakery was afraid of cancer. Even Hovan, who, despite his bachelor's degree, insisted cancer was a pharmaceutical company construct. Brendan had cancer already and breathed in deep floury lungfuls knowing it couldn't get worse. He even laughed at the letters; he looked happiest whenever a new one came. Ten years or so ago, he had gone into surgery and come out half a lung lighter. None of the doctors could make heads or tails of the tumor they had ripped out, and so began the journey of Brendan's lung. Sent from lab to lab, we would get letters from all the different labs, always the same thing: results inconclusive, forwarding your bio sample to such and such research station or university. I think Brendan started a stamp collection. I think he was a little jealous, too, of the lung fragment. It got to travel across the country; he had to work 108 hours a week, all the while still breathing death.

It was the flour, or the powdered sugar, or the asbestos that had once insulated and now scared the bakery workers. We tried not to think about it. We turned the radio on and let mindless songs wash over us. We talked about the past or the present, never the future. We told each other and ourselves that we were fine. The letters kept coming in.

Brendan's father died—cancer. It was he who had opened the bakery sixty years ago, and after sixty years, it had killed him. I was working when we got the call. I was washing dishes, Brendan was putting chocolate frosting on an eight-inch marble, and the phone rang. It took a minute for me to realize something was wrong. The radio was on, the sink was sloshing. I turned to see the eight-inch marble cake fly across the room and crash into the oven. I was speechless, motionless. Brendan ripped the radio's cable from its socket; it flatlined. He left.

I was washing chocolate frosting off the oven when the mail came in. More medical mail, the tumor had reached California, I wondered how long he had left. In the silent bakery, I wondered how long I had too.

death the chef

Emily Dorffer

Preparing blackened boy, I heat a house
with matches struck by boredom. Hungry flames
escape and gnaw the door. The boy can't douse
the fire that licks the walls and ends his games.

I marinate a girl in salty brine.
As coral traps her foot, some kelp and weeds
entangle legs. A shark's sharp teeth confine
her thrashing limbs. She trails from jaws and bleeds.

Methinks it's best to serve outdoorsmen chilled.
As snowflakes season skin, the hiker slips.
The crack of bone on stone announces spilled
ingredients, and frostbite tints his lips.

One day, dear reader, you shall make a fine,
delicious dish, and I alone shall dine.

addendum

Deon Robinson

the railroad track no longer shines,
draped in a destitute coat of rust.

barbed edges, a sight for scraping eyes.
the track braces for the landing of a flaring cardinal

sitting perched on the track's edges
mocking the world, compacted red like bullet wounds.

makes a tour spot of the wreckage
until it no longer feels welcome and darts away.

never so much as glance back
I remember abandonment is a symptom in all species.

ocd and heartbreak

Linzy Rosen

Pills line my dresser
Like tallies in a prison cell
Plastered on the walls
Counting down the days until liberation.
I organize my pills into neat rows and columns
Just another one of my OCD perks
Except the only one that is cute is my cleanliness
You said
Apparently my disorder can be picked apart by Notes and Retweets—
You clicked the share button.

I shake up each bottle
A melancholy melody to accompany my broken-record thoughts
I wash my hands over and over in the fiery breath of scorching water at
the thought of you
As red skin peels off
Like my clothes did that time in your bed
I guess I was too much to handle for more than one night.

My favorite pill is the one that looks like an atomic bomb
But whose name still sounds less foreign than yours when it rolls off my
tongue.

My raw hands glide across the wondrous curves of the child lock cap I
twist

Would you appreciate my body as much as this?
My hand fits better with the pill bottle than it did with yours.

Saliva embraces the pill as I gently slide it in the back of my throat
A euphoric reunion
How nice it is to be this close to something that will not push me away
That will not slam doors in my face or treat me like an experiment.

My fingers gingerly caress each tiny body
As I dump the remaining pills in my hand
They dance across the crosshatches of my palms and scars on my wrists
Softer than any kiss I've ever received.

A smile warped with incredible pain and a feeling I cannot yet detect
Crawls across my face
When I realize that
This is the most intimate experience
I've ever had.

synecdoche

Sophie Panzer

They say the painter Van Gogh
cut off his ear in a fit of tortured

madness and presented it to a prostitute
he might have loved, as if to say,

take this, make of me what you will,
derive my essence from this fragment

of flesh. Again and again we see
the blurred divide between madness

and genius. Think: what if, rather than
relying on endless testing and paperwork

colleges asked applicants for a single sliver
of belly or buttock or breast

mailed overnight in a cooler
and then, along with thousands

of others, fed through
a machine that could distill from it

every drip of ambition
every particle of desire

every tremor of weakness
as if the number of times you decided

to watch Netflix and eat ice cream
rather than study for AP Calculus

was configured deep in your tissues, mapped
in the intricate alignment of your cells.

honeyed

Sarah Blair

If my curls could talk, I know they'd say
"I love you, Mama"
The night sky knots cover my scalp like a hive,
protecting their queen. My strands crisscross back as
far as my roots: over blood and chains
and homes and frames and seas and my dad:
standing with his hat in hand, rubbing his eyes
saying "How was your day?"

they could see themselves

Arden Yum

The watercolor sky of each seemingly endless June day bled into the next. The sun turned the other girls red and left their skin bruised and tender. They slathered on aloe vera and emptied cans of spray-on sunscreen, but flakes of flesh still ended up on the front porch and in the bathroom sink. I did the same; smeared on layers of protection against the angry sun, anxiously waiting for my skin to get burned too. I felt the suffocating weight of warm air on my face and a stream of water droplets rushed from the roots of my hair to the back of my neck, but the pain did not come. Instead, I glittered in the sunlight and could see my pale skin darken into the sweet honey of summer. The sunscreen I had used to guard myself dripped away until my body shifted into shadow.

Two girls posed for a picture on the front steps of the bunk. I drifted into a corner and pretended to reorganize the pairs of sneakers lined up by the door. My head swiveled around periodically, waited for a half-second to be invited into the exclusive photoshoot, then went back to occupying myself with more arbitrary tasks. The girls held clenched, closed-mouth smiles. They stuck their elbows out and threw their shoulders back. Their arms were wrapped around each other, but one girl's fingers barely grazed the other's back. They stood perfectly still while drops of sweat collected into shallow puddles on the ground. After a single click of the shutter, their shoulders slumped back down. They started to fake laugh for a second pose and soon their forced giggles grew into uncontrollable laughter. Another click. One girl rushed around to the back of the camera to see what she looked like.

She let out a high-pitched cry for help. Her voice was burdened by the agony of summer heat and the insecurities she tried so hard to suppress.

She hated the way that her eyes narrowed into dark slits whenever her smile was genuine. She complained to her friend that it made her look *Asian*. She said *Asian* like she was spitting out rotten food. The disgust in her voice sent an earthquake through my spine. Could she see me? Did it matter? I stood speechless on the porch. Her words took refuge inside of my mind. My tan skin blended into the wooden walls, and I hoped that if I closed my eyes she wouldn't be there when I opened them. I stopped adjusting the shoes and kicking the dirt into piles. I walked into the corner of wet towels and bathing suits and tried to take up as little space as possible. Thick teardrops rolled down my cheeks, but I couldn't lift my hand high enough to wipe them away.

The sun dried my tears and left thin lines of salt on my face. I positioned my head toward the shade so my eyes wouldn't squint. Every muscle moved with calculated caution. I stared at my arms. Now they looked like they had been muddied, and no matter how hard I scrubbed, the layers of contaminated skin refused to fall off. I ran my fingers across my eyelids and failed to find the same deep-set eye creases and long lashes that the other girls had. I silently cursed the sun for making me different. They were beautiful in a way that I could never be. Yes, they burned. But they burned together.

As the day faded into night I sat on the front porch and watched streams of girls walk by and gossip and giggle. One girl's face blurred into another whenever I took a second to blink. They didn't need to look at their arms or trace their eyelashes. They could see themselves by watching each other. There was a security in their sameness, but they paid no attention to it. Some girls sat down next to me to see the stars, and I half smiled at them. Their eyes were pointed in every direction but somehow avoided contact with mine. I retreated into the darkness. In the midst of our closeness, I was still inevitably alone. The sun rose the next morning, and my fingers trembled because they were scared to touch the light.

dull

Jayla Stokesberry

The chair in the principal's office is so soft that if you sit there for long enough, you can sink into it and never resurface again. That's what happened to John Burkley. He went into the office, sat down in that plush chair, and they strapped him in there and yelled at him until he disappeared forever. Rumor has it that the principal sends him food once a week to keep him alive, with no one to talk to but the dust bunnies.

This is the third time that I've been asked to sit in the chair and speak to the principal. Each time before, I've managed to avoid that terrible fate, but it has only gotten harder to escape. I fiddle with my thumbs. No one has ever talked to the principal three times in one year and remained unchanged by the experience.

I sit in the waiting room until a student exits the office, seemingly unscathed. He paces toward his next class with his head down. He looks like a new transfer. A sad smile forms across my face. He'll learn.

"Next," the principal calls through the crack of the closing door. I push it open with the palm of my hand and enter the room.

The chair is older than I remember. The bright yellow fabric has faded to a brownish mustard color, and the stuffing is beginning to come out of it. I peer through one of its holes to look for John, but before I can find him, the principal motions for me to hurry, so I sit down and face her desk.

"Welcome, Jason," the principal says. "I suppose you know why you're here."

I glare at her. I'm not going to give in that easily. The chair supports my weight.

The principal clears her throat. I still don't answer.

"You, young man, are failing your classes. I've called you in to discuss your options. You seem to need a little extra . . ." She pauses. "Help."

"I don't need your help," I mutter.

"Your teachers have told me otherwise. I've been informed that you haven't completed a single assignment in several weeks. Is there a reason you've neglected your studying?"

"It must have slipped my mind," I answer.

She gives me a skeptical look, which I don't find entirely fair. I did forget about the assignments, at least, after I shoved them down the paper shredder.

She lets her suspicions go, though, and continues. "Jefferson Preparatory has a 100 percent pass rate. We have a wide variety of resources to help failing students—"

I interrupt her. "John was failing. Did you help John?"

"We have no records of any 'John' at this school."

That's a lie so glaringly obvious that she knows she has to correct herself.

"I suppose you are talking about Jonathan," she says.

"Burkley. Jonathan Burkley."

"Jonathan Burkley was removed from our program for tarnishing our reputation and refusing to obey guidelines—a path you may be headed toward if you are not careful, Jason."

The chair has begun to sink beneath me. I can almost feel John banging his fists against the inside of the chair in frustration.

"Luckily," she continues, "the staff here at Jefferson is willing to provide you with several options to assist with the learning process until you have fully adjusted to our rigorous climate."

"What if I never adjust?" I ask.

She stares right at me. No, she stares *through* me. Her gaze pierces through my chest and locks on to the chair behind me. She remains silent for a while, attaching my torso to the chair backing with two long metal skewers, and I wonder if she's going to leave me hanging here forever.

"Don't worry," she says finally. "You'll adjust, one way or another."

She blinks once, and the skewers disappear from my chest. My full weight rests upon the seat once again, but this time, my rear sinks completely beneath the fabric. I try to push myself back up with my hands, but it's impossible. I'm stuck.

"Now, do you have any more questions, or may we proceed?"

I decide to stay silent.

"Good," she says. "Let's discuss your options."

She opens a drawer and pulls an old leather book onto her desk. She blows on the book to clean it, and the specks of dust float towards me and dance around my vision. She's like a witch, casting spells on me, trying to transform me into a frog or a snake or some other type of slimy creature that she could take home as a pet.

She opens the book and reads from it silently. While she's distracted, I try to escape the grip of the chair again, but the more I try to loosen its grasp, the further I sink in. My body folds into a slight V shape. I sigh. I figure I'll have to wait until the principal decides to let me go.

The principal looks up to find that I've fallen further below the surface of the chair, and I swear I can see her lips form a tiny smirk.

"Jason," she says, "if you follow these steps, we will be able to get you out of this *situation* without problems."

Get on with it, I think. I don't dare to say it out loud.

"With your signature, I can write a recommendation for our two-step preparation program. The first step is the questioning."

"Questioning? What kind of questioning?" I don't like where this conversation is headed.

"When first joining our school," she explains, "many students partake in activities that are detrimental to our learning environment. Usually, students end all involvement in these activities within their first month here at Jefferson. Occasionally, a few students slip through the cracks. When students interfere with the learning environment, it is necessary to find the root cause so that it can be fixed. The questioning method has proven to be very effective."

It's true. No one at Jefferson Preparatory throws parties, does drugs, or cuts class. I've never seen anyone do even so much as blink during instruction time; everyone writes their notes in neat little columns without ever taking their eyes off of their teacher. They raise their hands to give insightful comments or, every so often, to throw a softball question to a teacher so that he feels good about answering it and being helpful. Then, they go home and all they do is sit at their desks with their homework for hours. There are no sports teams, no art club, no amateur rappers who think that they're famous because they got three hundred views on YouTube. There are only students, their worn-down pencils, and a desk lamp that never gets turned on because everyone's asleep by sundown. Working here is every teacher's dream.

"So you'll question me, and then what? What's the second step?" I ask. The chair gradually pulls me in further.

"You've heard of our training programs, haven't you?"

I ball my fists. "Training program" is a horrific euphemism.

You see, every once in a while, you'll get a kid who's slow to give everything up. Maybe he's a street basketball prodigy and his parents sent him here because the colleges won't offer him a spot on their team until he gets his grades up. He thinks he can juggle two things at once, so he spends his days playing ball with his friends, and he stays up too late at night trying to get his work done on time. He only has to nod off once during class for the teacher to send him to the principal's office. They'll have a discussion, and she'll write out a recommendation for a "training program" in New York. He won't be in class for a week or two. No one will notice.

When he comes back, he's just like the rest of them: staring at the whiteboard with soulless eyes. His school calls his parents to inform them of their child's success, and they are elated that their son can finally chase his dream. Except then he tells them that he doesn't want to play basketball anymore. He thinks it's a waste of time.

Eventually, the other streetball players show up at his house asking where he's been. They walk up the stairs, open the door to his room, and see a student hunched over a desk, filling out assignments with mechanical precision, and several dull pencils that have rolled onto the floor. He doesn't even look up. Without saying a word, they leave him there. That isn't the kid they're looking for.

No one knows what happens during the training programs. Maybe they're full of unlicensed surgeons who sever brains into pieces with their scalpels, or maybe they hire psychologists to strap students down to chairs and hypnotize them into robots. Only one thing is certain: the training programs change people. The principal ships you off to another state like she's returning a defective product back to a factory, and in a couple of weeks, they'll fix it for her and send it back free of charge. I don't want to be fixed. All I want to do is tell the principal that she can shove her training programs right up her—

But I don't say that. The chair would hear me. Instead, I tell her, "I'm not signing anything. I'm not doing the training program."

"Jason, we have training programs all across the country. We can find the right fit for you. All you have to do is sign some papers. Just say the word, and I'll bring them to you."

"I'm not doing it."

"Jason." She looks at me pointedly.

"You said I have options. I want to hear my other options."

"Jason!" She slams her fists against her desk. My lower body swings beneath my torso, and I start to fall until the fabric reaches up to my armpits.

"Don't you understand? You have no other options, Jason. It's the training program or the chair."

I start to wonder if it even matters anymore, because whether I drown inside of the chair or the principal sucks my soul out of my body, "Jason" will never be seen at this school again.

"What if I choose the chair?" I ask.

"You'd be the first."

"You're wrong," I say. "John did it too."

She sneers. "John doesn't exist. We made him up to scare kids like you into submission. It's easy to make an example out of someone that isn't real."

"Liar!" I say. "You're a liar!" With every word, the chair pulls me further into its fabric. My shoulders are completely smothered, and my neck sprouts above the seat like a pathetic little weed.

"No one at Jefferson would ever sacrifice themselves for some noble cause," she says. "Look around you. Does this look like a school of martyrs?"

I think of all the dull, monotonous faces I've passed by in the hallways, the perfectly aligned rows of desks in every classroom, the pristine school bathrooms, the deafening silence in the cafeteria at lunchtime, and the resigned, shuffling footsteps of the new students after their first meeting with the principal. I come to a realization: it doesn't matter whether John exists or not because this school will never change.

The principal reads that thought right off my face. "That's right. Your idol can't help you now. It's time for you to sign the contract."

"No."

"What?"

"I said no." The principal can reprogram a thousand students to do her bidding, but I refuse to let her control me.

Her cheeks flush with anger. "Do you think anyone will care about your sacrifice? No one will even remember you."

"I'm not doing this so that they will remember me," I say. My neck is submerged. I tilt my head back so that I can say my final words. "I'm doing this so that you will."

And with that, I take one last look at her faltering expression, then sink below the surface.

It's dark. I can't breathe. It's mind-numbingly dark. It's dark like the soot on the floor of an abandoned coal mine. It's dark like the infinite depths of outer space. It's dark like twenty thousand feet below the ocean. It's dark like the gaping mouth of a man-eating giant. The dark is suffocating me. I can't breathe. My lungs writhe inside of my body. Thorns of fire pierce my chest. I can't breathe. Fear seeps into my blood like acid. Pure agony.

I would do anything, *anything*, for a single molecule of air.

I'm on top of the chair again. I'm gasping. Coughing. Heaving. The principal looks at her watch.

"Thirty-seven minutes," she says. "Impressive. I was beginning to think you wouldn't want to come up after all."

Air is the sweetest thing I have ever tasted.

She pushes a piece of paper and a pencil towards me. "Are you ready to sign this paper? Or do you want to spend more time with my chair? Maybe a weeklong vacation?"

I snatch the pencil from the desk and sign her contract. I can't go back there. I'm sorry.

The tip of the pencil breaks off as I finish.

Her smile chills the air. "I knew you'd come around eventually. Now, follow me. Let's begin the questioning." I get up from that wretched, ugly chair and do as she says. As I leave the room, I can almost hear John screaming and begging me to be the one to make his pain worthwhile.

The door closes behind me.

shock value

Henry Wahlenmayer

Madison, standing arms folded by the linoleum counter, watched Kyle eat another grubby fistful of Cheetos and lick the dust off his palm. His round face, splattered with grease, peered up at the TV. Some sort of marathon was on—*Power Rangers*—and Kyle's beady eyes hadn't left the screen for hours. It seemed inconceivable that her son cared more about fictional superheroes than he did about the melodrama unfolding outside. Kyle loved Lassie, right? The dog, not the movie. Kyle hated that movie. Not enough explosions.

She turned and caught a glimpse of her husband through the cracked window of their trailer. He was holding Grandpa Turner's gun, tears streaming down his face. Madison looked away. *That's how you do it,* she thought. She glanced back at her child. There was something distorted about it, the way this scene was unfolding—the crying outside contrasted with the sickly glow of their cluttered living room. And there Kyle was, unmoving. Why wouldn't he move?

She didn't want him to be sad, she told herself. She just wanted to *see* him be sad. But what she wanted, the hysterics and the breakdowns and the the screaming, that wasn't going to happen. The television was on.

It wasn't their fault. They just didn't have the cash to go to the vet to do it. Blame the economy, blame the president. It was cheaper this way. Still, it made her want to vomit when she looked at their flat-screen and saw all the money they could afford to waste on that piece of garbage. Deep in her gut, she had known that Rick's promotion was a temporary respite. Nothing ever went well enough for them. Besides, all they ever watched on it was *Family Feud* and the goddamn *Power Rangers*. Her child loved it, and she hated it more.

The boy finished the Cheetos and sucked his plump fingers clean. Kyle's eyes were small and beady and completely unmoving. She felt bile rise in her throat.

A bark came from the outside of the trailer. Rick's muffled cries soaked through the cracked tile.

She just wanted Kyle to care. She wanted to grab that fat face and push it against the window until his snot ran down the glass and tears welled up in its eyes and Kyle could see her husband, its father, blowing the dog's brains out. And she wanted that boy, that parasite, to cry because that'd at least prove that it was human, and that it cared about anything or anyone. She thought about doing it, she really did. But Madison didn't think she'd be able to forgive herself.

Sounds stopped trickling in from outside the trailer. She could picture her husband taking deep, even breaths, trying to swallow his emotions back into his stomach. Madison turned away. There was a yelp and a gunshot and then nothing but the birds, voices like wind chimes, nature correcting itself through music. With one misshapen finger, Kyle turned up the volume on the television.

Madison felt a tug at the corner of her mouth. Kyle didn't look away from the screen, didn't blink, because *Lassie* was just a movie and the dog was just a dog.

the law of conservation of mass

Malcolm Slutzky

it works like this:
things are never new—
just rearranged,
uncovered, broken
open. i was here
when the universe
unfurled & space
realized its
emptiness. i was here
when it bloomed.
a blooming. when
a small thing
becomes large
all at once & without
warning. we, of course,
do not understand
these types of things.
if you
think too hard
about it,
the law
does not account
for emptiness—
which did not exist
before fullness,

but can now be found
in all manner of
places. one summer,
i found an
emptiness.
it started in me
slowly
edges curling out
like the beginnings
of a flower. grabbing me
by the throat, stretching me
out & in. sometimes an
emptiness
is so large that a
thing becomes its
emptiness.

depending on
who you ask
i am a girl.
an empty one.
blooming.
blooming.

just not sad enough

Danielle Sherman

The rejection notice feels cold and heavy in my hands.

I sit in a chair outside Ms. Bates's office—Ms. Bates, the counselor and school newspaper editor. You wouldn't find a single comma out of place in those sports articles. So, in a way, I already know why I'm here. *You did this to yourself, didn't you?*

Once the tick of the analog clock has faded to white noise, the wooden door swings open, and Ms. Bates beckons me inside. I wipe my palms on my jeans as I sit in the plastic chair; Ms. Bates has a swivel chair, a testament to her superiority. The door clicks shut.

Ms. Bates is a short, brown-haired woman; it is easy to imagine her with two kids in college, maybe a boy and a girl, and their university stickers are definitely slapped on the bumper of her Subaru. Not that I've ever seen her car. She gives me one of those smiles so often found in educators who are convinced they can change kid's lives, but there's a bit of quinoa still stuck behind her incisor.

"Jess, how've you been? Thanks for coming in today," she says with the same stale sweetness as the lollipops in the glass bowl beside her nameplate.

"Mm-hmm," I say, because my heart's already beating fast.

Ms. Bates must have sensed my anxiety or seen the way I fiddle with the paper in my hand, because she sits down gently as if the two of us were on a teeter-totter. "Don't worry, honey, you're not in trouble," she tells me. "I just happened to see something I wanted to talk to you about. You know how I'm in charge of the school newspaper, right?"

"Yeah. It's really good," I say lamely. It's actually pretty bad.

I feel that prickling sting behind the lids that renders it difficult to sustain eye contact. When Ms. Bates opens up her desk drawer, my will flies faster than the weird kids who sprint to the cafeteria, and I finally break. My gaze shifts to the lollipops and their vibrant cellophane wrappers.

"Well, honey," Ms. Bates continues, "I read all the submissions the students send to the newspaper, and that includes the little writing contest we held last quarter. I read the entry you submitted. You like to write?"

Ms. Bates is not the baseball coach, so I truly wonder why she throws me curveballs instead of getting on with it. But I smile despite the little squirrel that's squirming around in my stomach, and my fingers fold the corner of the rejection notice. "I guess," I say. "Just for fun."

"It's always good to have a hobby. An outlet." Ms. Bates sagely nods behind the rims of the glasses she bought at Costco. "But when I was looking at your writing, I saw some things that concerned me."

"Oh." I glance down at the rejection slip, at the note that asked me to come see Ms. Bates Thursday during lunch. I had expected this to happen before I had even received it—I had expected this to happen as soon as I turned in that stupid story. But the part of me with pencil shavings for a spine still wants to tell her that I really am a good kid, that there is nothing strange going on, and there is no need to worry. I keep my mouth shut with an effort.

At last, Ms. Bates withdraws the papers from her open desk drawer and sets them between us gingerly, like the ink is gunpowder. "I want to talk with you about this," she says, "not to punish you but just to understand." She's going for the motherly warmth of a cozy hearth, but it feels more like the frying circuits of an overheated computer.

I stare at the papers and the sloppy staple holding them together. I had wanted to get the staple at a perfect forty-five-degree angle, but, as usual, things hadn't worked out the way I wanted.

Ms. Bates clears her throat and speaks to fill my silence. "Let's see here."

She looks at the typing slathered across the pages but doesn't actually read it. "Your story was about . . . pirates? In . . . space?"

"Mm-hmm. They go on an adventure."

"An *adventure*." I notice a slight raise of a penciled-in eyebrow. "With all kinds of *action*, I noticed. A swordfight. And the ending . . ."

"What is it?" I lean forward, eager to get this over with, but I can feel those pencil shavings at the same time, coalescing into a hard ball of lead. I am determined not to give in.

"Well, it's happy." Ms. Bates puts her thumb beneath her chin and an index finger over her lips, her features furrowed. "Your characters, they win the big battle. They end up friends, and all of them are alive. Do you see how a counselor like me would be worried about this?"

I shrug and shift lowered eyes to my name printed on the incriminating evidence. "I guess so. Doesn't mean anything, though. It was just an idea I had."

"I don't think so, Jess. To me, this sounds like a cry for help." She reaches out her hand as if to pat mine but stops just short for dramatic effect. "I've seen many teenagers call out to me through their writing like this. And as someone who cares about you, I don't want to ignore the warning signs."

"But there's nothing wrong with me, really. Just what's so off about it in the first place?" I demand, surprised at my own boldness. "What is so horrible about stories and fantasies?"

"It's just not . . . it's just not sad enough." Ms. Bates sighs, but I think she's excited to have a hard case to crack. I can tell she's secretly impressed with how artfully she extends her sympathy. "The other kids, you know, didn't write this kind of stuff," she says. "Sarah Williams wrote about high school heartbreak. Casey Johnson wrote about his abusive father. That's the kind of thing teens are *supposed* to write about. Those are the kinds of submissions the newspaper likes to receive."

"And you aren't concerned about *them*?"

"Of course not!" An impatient grin pulls at the woman's thin lips. "Kids are always filling up their pages with angst and darkness. That's what makes it art, isn't it? That's what makes it good!"

Ms. Bates waits expectantly for my enthusiastic reply, but I just cross my arms and stare at a stain in the floor carpeting. I was already familiar with this fact; I had read the newspaper countless times and marveled at how eloquently ninth-graders had described their depression in tear-smeared letters. Some pieces were even written entirely without capitalization—a real showstopper.

But I didn't understand—still don't understand—why suffering makes something more meaningful. Why despair makes something better written. The stubborn child inside of me, the one who appreciates a positive emotion every now and then, refuses to nod along with Ms. Bates. I can feel our teeter-totter rocking back and forth.

Still she is determined to convince me. "You are a good writer," Ms. Bates tells me, fishing for all the best movie lines she can remember, "but you could be a *great* one. There's just something missing, and it alarmed me, that's all. Usually I'll see at least one mention of a coffee shop to symbolize tortured artistry and loneliness or maybe some nostalgic flashbacks in italics. But I couldn't find any second person in your piece, and that sent up a big red flag."

"I was just trying to be unique," I say, nearing exasperation. "Kayla Dawson has published a sob-inducing little memoir about her eating disorder in the past *five issues*. I thought maybe happy could be new or interesting or powerful or—"

"But happy isn't deep." Ms. Bates shakes her head. She leans back in her swivel chair and laces her fingers like a therapist closing in on the eureka moment. "People always like some good oppression. The stories of all the emotionally damaged and internally conflicted children are just so *important*. Their voices deserve to be heard—or do you disagree?"

I realize that Ms. Bates is on the offensive now, and I have leapt right into the sugar-sticky mousetrap of that deceptively welcoming lollipop bowl. "No, I—" I shake my head vehemently, because God forbid I find those such-important stories too dramatic, too flowery, or too unoriginal. Those kids have already been through enough as it is. Could I dare disagree with stricken lamentations?

"Jess, I know the advertisement asked for short stories," Ms. Bates continues, eyes gleaming now that the kill is near, "but that doesn't mean fun little adventures anymore. At your age, excitement is shallow, and innocence is privilege, and standard narrative structure is just so *naïve*. Can't you think back on anything that made you cry or gave you trauma? Any racial or religious persecution? Not even a broken friendship? Because that's what impresses people—it makes you sound so very *intellectual*."

The fervor in her voice and the almost-wicked shine to her eyes warps Ms. Bates to resemble a rabid animal, if only for a second. In that moment, however, I feel a cold kind of dread that presses its clammy hand around me until I shrink into myself. Her words don't make sense to me, but a persistent thought, a hopeless desperation, prods the back of my mind. *You want to get published in the newspaper, don't you?*

"It's just that everybody's trying to make themselves seem different in the same exact way," I protest meekly.

Ms. Bates gives me playful, narrowed eyes; she knows she's already won. In the end, I am no match for her and her swivel chair. She might say this only goes to show that satisfying conclusions are the least interesting.

"I'll tell you what," she says, tapping a finger to my sorry excuse for prose. "I can see you're coming around, and I know you have real potential. We'll try an exercise to fix your mindset. I want you to give a second try at this submission, and maybe this time you'll see things in a new light."

I think about my name on the rejection notice, and then I mentally transfer it to the contributors' segment of the school newspaper. My words printed on pages other people will read, even if the words are slathered so thick with emotion you can't quite see the point underneath the shiny surface. I bounce my head lightly and offer a small smile without showing my teeth. I get off the teeter-totter and out of my chair, but I leave my story behind.

A day later, I sit with my notebook in my lap and chew on my pencil eraser, but instead of drawing doodles and constructing plot outlines, I close my eyes and pretend I'm a space pirate. Except I haven't won the grand battle; the enemy's cannons were just too loud, and their swords were just too sharp. I imagine that all my friends have been killed, all my treasure stolen, and all my hope extinguished—maybe that I even lost an eye, so I have to wear an eyepatch now.

Then I write about how sad and lonely I am, taking care to use second person when I'm actually referring to myself and including one-word paragraphs to showcase true flashes of genius. I throw a skull in there for a real edgy metaphor. When I'm done, I think I feel better. Like a real writer.

Still, the acceptance notice feels cold and heavy in my hands.

monophobia

Claire Shang

monophobia (the irrational fear of being alone)

she collects words. makes lists and pins them in her apartment. her walls
have long forgotten the color of her hair, her caving clavicle, her clattering
teeth. they have been blinded by the paper: mostly scraps, forced onto the
rough wallpapering. the walls, they resent her for covering their eyes.

(she knows this because they whisper while she's asleep.)

she is always writing. she has pens everywhere. extracting them from
behind her bookcases, buried in her sock drawer. you even find one pinned
on her wall.

why's that pen up there? you ask.

i was making a list of things that i can always trust, she says nonchalantly.

you don't ask: what about me? don't you trust me?

instead, you clear your throat and survey the wall that is weighted with
fluttering papers. it's like the whole wall is about to take flight.

adding quickly, she says that: i realized soon after i can't even always
trust a pen. the foreverness of their ink, the way it bleeds through the paper
desperately, trying to escape . . . but you know, once you make a list you
can't change it.

you didn't know this was a rule. but if she says it's one then it is. she's
always been good at these things. she's usually right.

you sit down at the coffee table. its surface is covered with shards of
paper laminated over with stained plexiglass. a splatter of dried coffee
covers the title of a list with four items: love money happiness fame.

pointing to it, keeping your index finger on the stain so the list won't
run away, you ask about the list delicately.

that silly little thing? she cries.

yeah, you shrug, trying to look disinterested. remember what the poster looked like in the counselor's office? disinterested: pupils that slither to the corners of eyes, raised eyebrows, hand on cheek.

it's a list of what people *think* you need in life but is actually complete bull, she says. i made it a while back.

oh.

and you're back to reading the lists. you finish reading the coffee table's surface, so you move on to the legs. there are four, but the lists are plastered on crookedly, words often left dangling, only to be finished on the next face of the leg.

she turns around, sees you crane-necked, and laughs hoarsely. the pawing of a pen against cheap paper, the sound of her rippling hair, the shreds of lists flapping against each other like a paper ocean. familiar sounds.

she tiptoes to reach the top of the wall. says nothing as she does so. neither do you.

buried deep under the sofa lies another layer of lists. these are personal and you're glad she's busy taping a new fleet of lists onto the ceiling so she can't see you absorbing everything. head half submerged in the dusty darkness, you find *unlucky numbers* (10—when the older kids, your role models, taught you about popularity and cafeteria lunch and magazine covers and ribcages, 12—when you feel gray all over for the first time, 15— when you're sitting with the gray on your birthday, no one else, just gray. everywhere.)

you army crawl deeper into the murkiness of the under-couch. here you find *dreadful colors* (*stained white*—the color of bathroom tiles and toilet bowls and office walls, *ocean blue*—the color of your eyes trapped into one dimension, *gray*—how loneliness feels, all scratchy and hollow and damp.)

she's done taping the lists up. her pointed feet step down from the ladder and land lightly on the plexiglassed lists on the ground.

where are you? she asks quietly.

you scramble to read more, absorb more, even though you know this is knowing too much of her.

reluctantly you roll out, yelling boo with lackluster energy, coated with dust.

you found my secret spot! she says, flustered.

you push yourself up with your arms and sink into the couch, causing dust to ricochet off the cracked leather.

you notice that in your absence, the whole ceiling has been plastered down with lists. you spot *beautiful words, best days of the week,* and *most populated countries.* a thicket of paper whispers around you.

you stand up, knees trembling, large eyes, confused eyes. all four walls are lined with lists. the ground is too. the tables, the bar counter, the fridge. and the ceiling.

you spot one last list resting cockily by the mirror: *worst places to be trapped in.*

the only item is: *your own brain.*

as soon as you look up, the ceiling comes crashing down in a fitful plume of smoke and crackled cement. as you emerge from the rubble with plaster and slips of paper on your arm, you notice that she is gone. and so are the endless lists with their endless words.

so it's just you now. just you.

mass production of flames

Marriya Schwarz

For the third time in my eight-hour shift, the needle pricks the scabbed and clotted skin outlining my fingernails. Grimacing slightly, I lift my fingers from the soft cotton blouse and watch the crimson liquid pool over my cuticles. Bringing my hands to my cream-white apron, I add to the decorations of scarlet scattered around the cloth. I have to be careful. Mr. Blanck and Mr. Harris don't like it when blood gets on the shirtwaists. I don't want to explain to my family why we won't be eating this week. Usually, the bosses don't spend their time in the lower levels; the salty stenches of blood and sweat tend to turn people away. Sponging the sweat off my forehead with my wrist, I try to stay focused on the task at hand.

Still, my mind continues to wander. It doesn't help that people are hollering, enjoying their Saturday afternoons eight floors below. I can imagine myself wearing one of these shirtwaists and strolling through the streets. My sister is always going on and on about getting one of those lavish hats to balance on the top of her head, feathers and flowers spilling from it. Shaking the fantasy from my head, I glance over at the big clock hoisted above the door. Only twenty minutes left, and no mistakes now. That's what Mr. Blanck is always telling us. As the uniformed men brought in the new electric machines, he told us specifically, wagging his finger in our faces, "Three thousand stitches a minute. No mistakes."

I count to six thousand before I glance at the clock again. Only a minute and a half has gone by. My pride tugs at the corner of my lips as I realize that I have beaten the average already. Feeling my mind start to wander yet again, I shift in my seat. The bosses make us pay for our own electricity, so I need to keep focused. There can be no wasting it. No matter how bad the working conditions are, everyone who quits always comes back within the next week, like a boomerang. With the current economy, we need to take any job we can get.

The sweat trickles down past my ear, overflowing like a crashing waterfall, as I try to focus on my stitches. However, my sewing machine neighbor constantly shifting in her seat is distracting me. She's just a child of ten years old. I can tell that she needs to use the bathroom, but with the foremen watching, there are no bathroom breaks. Their silent rubber heels always catch people and send them back to their stations, pursed lips hidden beneath their groomed moustaches.

I count to 15,096 when the smell of smoke wafts into my nostrils. My mind tries to play it off as exhaustion-induced hallucination. However, when I glance back over to my neighbor, I see her own nose scrunched up at the odor. Everyone is so attached to their work and the money it brings in that they don't even bother to look for the source. The foreman is too busy scolding a young German girl about her needles that he doesn't even look up. Seeing as I am ahead on my stitches, I risk a glance behind me. A wisp of smoke is exiting from the tips of a rag bin. Before my eyes, I watch that same wisp turn to red and yellow as the flames leap upward.

"Fire!" I shout, the word ripping from my throat before I even realize that the noise is coming from me. The other English-speaking girls' heads whip upwards, leaping from their machines.

"Fuoco!" an older Italian woman nearby shouts. Soon, every translation of the word is springing up along the eighth floor. By now, the flames are leaping across the room, licking at our ankles.

With the recent union protests in our building, Mr. Harris took it upon himself to lock all of the exits except for the Greene Street stairway. There, he would force us to undergo bag checks to make sure we weren't stealing extra thread or needles in our purses. Only he has the keys to the other exits that he carries on a large brass ring.

As we press closer to the other side of the room, I watch as the foreman tries to use the hose to dampen the fire. However, the valve is rusted shut from lack of use. The doorway to the Greene Street stairway isn't even visible anymore. The smoke completely covers it, blanketing over our only escape from top to bottom. Wicker baskets are scattered around the room in chaos. The fire just continues to eat them up, its hunger still not satisfied.

Blindly, I look around for my little sister, trying to catch a glimpse of her red braids somewhere in the crowd. I'm still calling out her name frantically when a small hand grips ahold of my dress. Quickly, I turn around to see my Ann staring back at me. Her cheeks are red; tears flowing freely down the sides of her face. The bottoms of her dress are singed, like she barely made it out before the flames took hold of what they thought they were entitled to. Her breath escapes her lips raggedly as her smaller hand tangles with mine. I give it a short squeeze, and we push toward the elevator shaft. Already, girls are piling in, trying to cram as many bodies as they can into one car.

"No more!" A girl barks at the rest of us, closing the gate quickly behind her. The last thing I see of her is the soot draped beneath her cheekbones as the shaft descends downward.

"We didn't get on that one," Ann murmurs, her bottom lip quivering.

"Next one, Annie, next one," I whisper back, tugging on her hand. I can tell she's terrified, her tears dropping onto the floor next to her feet. "Remember our plans? We are going to become rich and wear fancy evening gowns—"

"Can I get a fancy hat?" she asks me, suddenly.

"The fanciest," I assure her.

"A purple hat?" she asks again, her voice trembling.

"The brightest, biggest purple hat we can find." I nod to her. The next car never arrives. People start to become frantic, pushing forward and trying to see what the holdup is. The people up in front are whispering to the back that the elevator has crashed and there will be no more. Screams flood my ears as people jump down the shaft to escape the fire that is drifting even closer to our bodies that are shivering even though we aren't at all cold.

"Come on." Ann tugs on my hand and urges me closer to the shaft.

"We aren't jumping, Annie," I tell her, urgency etched in my voice.

"Everyone else is doing it."

"We'll die on impact," I try to convince her, but she is having none of it. Instead, she pushes to the front of the group. I get caught in the back, angry girls in scorched dresses covering up her trail. I try to yank a girl backward to get back to my sister, and she kicks me straight in the knees. Hobbling for a few seconds, I at last get to the front of the group. Ann is standing at the very edge of the shaft. I try to pull her back, but I only get the back of her necklace that we made together when we were children. Beads fly down with her as I clench my eyes closed, as if that will block out her scream. For a second, I can't breathe. My sister is gone, and I don't wait to hear the crash landing. I took this job to keep my family alive, and I failed. Without her, it just seems all over. With my knees aching, I limp to the back of the crowd.

My vision is foggy from my own tears, but I run back toward the fire escape. Girls are standing around the window, watching the fire trucks pull in outside. They are screaming, their words overlapping so it sounds like a foreign tongue I've never heard before. I watch as the ladders fall short and the flames grow taller. Taking a deep breath, I think of my other family members. With our mother sick, they still need me to help provide a somewhat steady source of income. With their survival on my mind, I push my way to the front.

My first steps on the fire escape are wobbly. I don't feel completely safe on the thing, but then again, I don't feel at all safe in the building either. Other girls are screaming at me for running past them, but in the moment, I don't care. Beneath my feet, I can feel the rumble of the girls in front of me, scrambling down. Quickening my pace, I throw my shoes off, figuring

I can do this quicker barefoot. The metal is hot beneath my skin, which gives me an incentive to run faster. I'm just at the second floor when the fire escape releases a fatal creak. Clenching my teeth together, I run faster before the metal caves out from beneath me. Clattering to the ground, I'm lucky that I'm at a short enough distance that the net the firefighters have set up catches my fall. Others are not so fortunate.

As I'm rolled off of the net, I try not to pay attention to the falling figures or the disheveled tangles of hair. But I can't do anything to block the screams.

A week later, I am called back to collect my paycheck from that terrible day. My heart is still in pieces, the remnants of my sister's necklace coiled around my wrist. They place both of our paychecks in my hands. As soon as I get the money, I turn back around and walk toward a store that Ann and I only dreamed of entering. And I buy a hat. Not just any hat. The fanciest purple hat that they have.

ice cream

William Blomerth

The room was quiet and still, and I would have thought myself deaf if it hadn't been for the buzzing and whirring of the machines keeping my aunt alive. I hadn't even known rooms could be so dark until that night, and the only window in the room let in the deeper darkness of the night. The silence itself was remarkable, achieved by a room crowded with bodies. Heat radiated from the bodies and made the room stuffy and suffocating. Everyone in the room was waiting for death. My aunt was lying on the bed that was more hardware than cushion, and many people who loved her were standing and sitting in various parts of the room. The room was definitely too small to hold all of the love . . . or the sadness.

ALS, or Amyotrophic Lateral Sclerosis, is a degenerative nerve disease that slowly and viciously kills its victims. My mother's side of the family carries the ALS gene, and Auntie Chi Chi had developed the disease. My mother had taken care of her for as long as we could at our house, but in the final weeks of her life, we knew she would have to stay in a nursing home. I watched as my aunt, the energetic sales rep glued to her cell phone, became a wisp of a human body that could barely say anything. I had seen her spirit leave her eyes. She was not ready to die; she was too young and loved life too much. Everyone in the darkness that night realized the same thing: the end was near.

While privately mourning, I remembered my first-hand experience with my aunt and her lack of basic motor skills. My mother and father were busy preparing a medication in the kitchen, which was serving as a pharmacy. My task was to feed my aunt ice cream. This was the same ice cream the rest of the family ate, no special medications or supplements, just a creamy vanilla. I put the ice cream in a bowl, a bowl that we had all used for years. I grabbed a spoon, not a special feeding tool for the sick, a spoon that I had used countless times before. I sat in front of her, perhaps the only ill relative of mine who hadn't been ready to die when it was time. Taking a spoonful of ice cream, I guided it toward her mouth. This was a mouth that could barely speak anything besides what must be described as a moan, let alone eat with much success. She opened her mouth, and I inserted the spoon. I saw her molasses-like lips close around the spoon, and I gently pulled back, as if I were feeding a baby. She had taken just a little off of the top. We went on like this, and we couldn't even get halfway through the dessert before the ice cream had melted.

I knew no young child in my parents' eyes would be charged with the duty of feeding the sick. My playroom had been long gone as well; my old toys were moved out and replaced with a bed and various medical accessories to keep first my grandmother (a victim of cigarettes) and then my aunt alive. I realized I was becoming a young adult. I was a twelve-year-old growing up alongside the diseases and sicknesses that had taken two family members in quick succession.

I struggled to keep the ice cream off of her face, realizing what my aunt had to go through. She couldn't even have ice cream without getting it dribbled down her chin. Ice cream, a universal symbol of happiness and glee, was an arduous task for her to consume. I thought of the kind of happiness it must have brought her when she was my age and younger; images of little kids running around playfully after the ice cream truck ran through my mind. I thought of the joy ice cream had brought me in previous years. I thought of Maya, Chi Chi's daughter, who so enjoyed ice cream. My God, her daughter: How would she survive the years after her mother's death? How would she deal with a motherless house? What was being imprinted in her brain at this moment, watching her mother slowly die? What would be left in my mind after this was all over? Would it ever really be over? These thoughts made me sick as I stared at the melted ice cream, and when we were done, I pushed the bowl away as if I could distance myself from these feelings.

That night in the nursing home, amongst the silent darkness, I came to my epiphany. My aunt would die soon, but it was okay. She was going to enjoy the heaven that she believed in much more than this life. Her long-term suffering, pain, and embarrassment (terrible for her Japanese pride) would finally come to an end. She would fly higher than the superficial world of today, escape the chains of her diseased body, escape the nursing home she despised so much, say farewell to the crowd of loved ones in her room, fly past my inescapable feelings, and be reunited with wherever the spirit of her parents went. I knew Maya would soon come to the same realization and the love in the room would guide her to this eventually. Chi Chi would die with those she loved on Earth all around her, and she wouldn't have asked for more.

allegro vivace

Jessica Lao

blue still life

Velda Wang

flower study

Shannon Horton

holiday lights

Austin Li

paramnesia

Noelle Hendrickson

untitled

Devika Sharma

staircase

Daniel Marquez

three apples

Alexandra Bowman

yellow leaf

Chris Howard

the required writing supplement section

Caleb Pan

—The Required Writing Supplement Section—
Every student has a unique life experience and a set of circumstances by which they are shaped and influenced. Your background may have been shaped by family history, cultural traditions, race, ethnicity, religion, politics, income, ideology, gender identity, or sexual orientation.

Reflect on a time when you had to relate to someone whose life experience was very different from your own. How did you approach the difference? If put in a similar situation again today, would you respond differently? If so, how? (650 word limit)

When I was in third grade, I was picked as part of a team to represent my school at a brain bowl. My team only placed second, which is why I did not include it on my application.

I befriended a participant from another school, who I will call Throckmorton to preserve racial and ethnic ambiguity. Throckmorton was a Muslim, indicated by a pinback button he wore that read "I am a Muslim." At the time, I wore a handmade LEGO cross necklace (with a rare barbed-wire ring accessory as an attached piece to represent the crown of thorns which I was very proud of). He was certainly different, but he liked LEGOs too, so he was a cool kid.

The host school provided pre-made lunches with no exchangeable options. Unfortunately for Throckmorton, the main course was a ham sandwich. He felt bad for wasting food by throwing out the ham, but I intervened to absolve his conscience. In my theological opinion, a nice perk of Christianity over the other Abrahamic faiths is that we're allowed to eat whatever we want. So, to emulate the self-sacrifice and love of Christ, I offered to eat it for him.

"Wait! God lets me eat ham!"

Throckmorton perked up and exclaimed, "You're a good friend!"

After the brain bowl, Throckmorton introduced me to his parents. Before I could introduce him to my parents, he had to go, and I never saw him again. If I were in a similar scenario today, I would also eat someone's food in the Lord's Name. Amen.

Please briefly explain and elaborate on an extracurricular activity or work experience that you were unable to include in your application. (200 word limit)

One of my most beloved memories is of waking one spring morning, fully refreshed and to the chirping of birds. It has been a while since either has happened.

I have noticed a cultural and byzantine leaderboard for sleep deprivation. I hypothesize contestants use hours of lost sleep to approximate their fortitude. The most prestigious claim I have heard came from a classmate who allegedly stayed awake for seventy-two consecutive hours by instilling his bloodstream with caffeine and Xanax. He eventually dropped the class—he's probably dead.

For my entire life, I have been an activist opposing this disillusioned award system. I boast an average contribution of 8 hours/day, 7 days/week, 52 weeks/year for over fifteen years. Admittedly, it has been difficult in recent years with other lesser commitments conflicting with my participation, but I plan to continue my passionate work into higher education.

I am dedicated to sleep because it embodies the inevitability of imperfection. I accept the necessities of resting and revitalizing are quintessential to true satisfaction. To sleep is to take care of yourself and not to run a race to nowhere.

I wrote this at 2 a.m.

Describe a specific situation or activity in which you made a meaningful difference and contribution in the lives of others through your effectiveness as a leader in which the greater good was your focus. Discuss the challenges and rewards of making your contribution. (500 word limit)

In third grade, I was educated in the Montessori model: a classroom designed to cultivate curiosity and open discovery, an organic approach to education.

The greatest mystery of our time was simple: Where do babies come from?

The most common theory was that babies were spontaneously grown in mothers' stomachs. I, however, was not satisfied. There was a large visual encyclopedia in the classroom; big books with lots of words were the ultimate and credible sources of truth. I consulted the tome, hoping it might elucidate the origins of life. I studied the anatomy section until I came across the reproductive system.

It took ten minutes of critical thinking and deducing to differentiate and understand the functionality of the organs depicted by artistic diagrams. I also educated myself in the concept of puberty, recognizing some key components in human conception were unavailable at my age. Finally, the description of copulation was bizarre, but I was able to cognitively assemble the act.

Eureka! The speculations and conjectures were over—knowledge such as this was power. I was the natural leader in the class (by default because I was abnormally large) and saw it as my duty to enlighten my classmates.

Some were in shock, most likely traumatized; others nodded with interest, quick to accept the big book as evidence. The enigma was no more.

However, the encyclopedia described intercourse simply as an insertion followed by a deposit. We assumed an accurate analogy was like filling a car with gas. This left us with further questions. *What was the duration of the deposit? Does it start upon insertion? How does the body know when to cease deposit? Or does the female have a responsive capacity limit?* After many discussions with car analogy–based theories, we finally came to the teacher and asked if she could provide any insight. She responded by banning all discussion on the subject and removed the encyclopedia from the classroom. *The suppression of knowledge! How tyrannical!* I led a protest to bring back the encyclopedia, explaining our aims and progress.

Our teacher reconsidered, then relented on the condition we remain quiet on the newfound topic. Keeping our word, with the promise we'd eventually get our answers, the encyclopedia was returned with me as its gatekeeper.

With that, I launched an era of scientific fascination, our teacher happily facilitating and catering to the interests we found in the encyclopedia. The renaissance eventually deteriorated when I lost interest and started writing, the class losing its pioneer. I don't know where my classmates are right now, but I can say with proud certainty that I left a lifelong impact on every single one of them.

Has there been a time when you've had a long-cherished or accepted belief challenged? How did you respond? How did the challenge affect your beliefs? (500 word limit)

Once, I was procrastinating by stumbling through an endless chain of linked Wikipedia articles. I started with the Indian caste system and eventually came across the International Flat Earth Conference. This event piqued my interest. I shared the event's website with several peers for their valued opinions. My so-called friends, the intolerant rabble, mocked the astrophysics minority. I was heartbroken at how frivolously they rejected an opposing view.

Although I had dismissed notions of a flat Earth in the past, I put my "globehead" principles aside to immerse myself in their society. Throughout my education, I was surrounded by globe representations and readily accepted them as the shape of the earth. Perhaps I did let myself be indoctrinated by mainstream media and NASA. It was uncomfortable to let a belief I held without question be challenged.

As I delved into the flat Earth community, I encountered a syndicate of conspiracy theorists, literalist zealots, and internet scum. It became apparent that comprehending this intellectual conglomerate, including their numerous ideological schisms, was near impossible.

My revelation? We are all people, people who have no idea what they're doing with their lives: I squandered my time gaining trivial knowledge from Wikipedia; they filled the void in their lives with nonsensical paranoia. I was unable to accept their beliefs, but it was a valuable lesson of how we are more alike than we are unalike.

That, and there are enough dumbasses for tickets at $249 per person to sell out.

Why do you want to attend [school name], and how do you think [school name] will prepare you to pursue opportunities in that field after graduation? (250 word limit)

I should say I want to sate my thirst for knowledge at *the caliber* you offer, to hone my unique talent and natural leadership under your *renowned programs*, and to enrich myself in your *vibrant community of creative and critical thinkers*. Listen, I don't want to do another four years. It's not just you—I mean I don't want to with anyone. I almost registered with the Peace Corps to avoid all the confrontation. You somehow found my email and address. I don't know who sold me out, but the way you cluttered my inbox and mailbox was unappreciated. Just because my parents like you doesn't mean I do. You were the one insisting that I take my time and make "the right choice for me." I'm not naïve, okay? I know you drip the exact same honeyed words to all us go-getter types: we're talented, we're unique, we're what you're looking for.

Am I that special? What am I really to you? You've said you want to know my interests, life stories, and plans to change the world. Be honest though—the first thing you see are my numbers, right? I'm not mad, I know you can't help it, but you should know that I know.

I'm sorry. I'm still young and inexperienced. I'm really trying to figure out what's best for me. I don't know if this is meant to be, but I'm willing to give us a chance. I await your response.

You may upload one optional supplemental resume for further consideration:
Uploaded: **AcceptanceLetterFromRivalSchool.pdf**

Thank you for your application!

fifteen months

Kate Bishop

What a beautiful thing
it was to have loved
the light in you.
It was a kaleidoscopic
tempest: crystalline fragments
of shattered glass
breaking against the hardwood floor
in a crescendo of
iridescence.
The remnants
of opals left to
glimmer unassumingly
on top of clovers in the
early morning are nothing more
than its distorted reflection
in a river during the rain.
If there was ever
an equivalent
to watching you wilt,
it is the incessant
torture
of your cold hands seizing
everything I want to say
and rearranging my words
into your name.

I'm only here because
you preferred oblivion.
My throat hasn't stopped hurting
for fifteen months,
six letters scratching it raw
whenever I even
think of them.

numbers

Patrick Erb-White

My life is full of numbers, which intrigues me a lot
I've been crunching these numbers, and this is what I got:
I added them together, and they all added up to you.
Either that, or I forgot to carry the 2.

Let's see.

I've had at least 3 crushes, 5 at most,
I have 2 blogs, 1 of which has only 4 posts.
3 favorite PC games, between which I've played
over 300 hours—about 12 and ½ days.
4 years of high school, of which I've completed 2,
then about 4 years of college—woohoo!
So, if I do the calculations right,
that's about 2,390 days and nights.

As far as dreams go, as far as I can recall,
only 3 have to do with you in any way at all.
I can't even remember 90% of my dreams, rounding down.
I've had 5 nightmares, 2 of them relating to clowns.
I write about 80% of my fiction based on dreams—well,
the dreams that are interesting, like 1 where I traveled to hell
(or the CGI equivalent).
7 days a week, 365 and a ¼ days in a year, which means
there's about 52 weeks a year, so it seems.

To convert that to seconds, if I may be so bold,
means I'm over 530 million seconds old.

Yes, I'm an old man, bet you didn't sign up for that,
but I think 505 million is where you are at.
But we're pretty young compared to the earth we are on,
whose life so far is, well, a number with 17 0's, seconds long.
(really puts things into perspective, doesn't it?)

299,792,458 m/s is the speed of light,
that's the universal speed limit—yeah, right.
You, my friend, are much faster than that;
you shoot down my questions before I even ask.
My crush on you, in terms of months, only lasted 4,
and since then have passed almost 19 months more,
and over the course of those 600 days,
you think I've moved on, hell, you think that I'm gay.
But, if I'm to let the truth be known,
I am just as I was before I met you: alone.

My life is full of numbers, a heck of a lot,
I've crunched all these numbers, and this is what I got:
They all add up to someone, anyone besides you,
and this time, I remembered to carry the 2.
(I highly doubt I messed up, but even then,
I don't want to go through all that again.)

like planting

Lucas Grasha

A writer writes
to rip a hole in a floor.
To find a bloom in a blight.

Because a poem startles the night
to puncture safety and its borders. It pours
into your dormant, furrowed brain to rewrite

patterns walked into the ground. Might—
vacant crucible—is like every board
rebuffing new blooms (the freight

of everything) and is exhumed. The tight
floor is safe and dying. Hoarded
seeds in the mind's cabinet ripen

like sediment. The writer rights
pestilent fallowness. Then: words
that abuse vacant troughs with light

and uprooting hands which fight
with manic pain to erase borders
from the mind's geography. At night,
the poem startles with fruitful blight.

to tullula

Heather Jensen

in the carnage across the road
lives a pod of film.
7.99 from the pharmacy, across
from the laundromat,
and i have left it
in carcasses
and skeletons
of foliage.

the travelers who live
behind the thicket of cactus
tell me of subway tile and redwood elevators
but soil takes my tongue
where the highway cuts through my mouth,
and the cicadas leave their skin outside
my bedroom window, where
the moon is
the cold end of an eraser.

opportunity has its own wheels and i either
make my own
or catch on
quick.

lessons from pot stock on living my life

Lilly Dickman

"What do you want to do in life?" My biggest fear is having to answer this question. My twin sister answers it with ease. Being twins, we're obviously the same age, so we've had the same amount of time on this Earth to come up with an answer to this question. Clearly, then, time isn't the independent variable in this equation. I don't know why we both couldn't have woken up one day with a light bulb above our heads.

"I want to go to film school in California so that I can live by the ocean and be a screenwriter. If that doesn't work out, I'll be a biochemical engineer," my sister answers in one breath. Her plan seems unrealistic, until she explains her web of filmmaking classes and independent studies, acting courses on top of AP Biology classes that seem to have been worked seamlessly into her schedule. In reality, her meticulous plan wasn't easy to configure. My sister worked through emails upon emails, meeting upon meeting, and summer school to achieve the arrangement of courses that will create the yellow brick road to her dream occupation.

Me, on the other hand—I can't even decide what I want from the sushi menu at dinner. Faced with any decision, especially about my future, I shut down. At a time when I'm preparing to make choices involving hopes and dreams, colleges and majors, my indecision is an issue. One day I think I should study psychology, the next I think I want to write, the day after that I want to own an overnight camp and live in the woods. I can't even decide who is the more "normal" one in this scenario, my decisive sister or wishy-washy me.

"Work hard, and you can achieve it," says pretty much every teacher, college counselor, or parent ever. *How am I supposed to work hard if I don't even know what I'm working for?* I think. I can't strive for it if I don't know what *it is. It's not fair,* I think. *Why do some people get to know what they want to do and not others?*

It seems to me that the people who know what they want to do from the beginning have an overarching better shot at life. The sooner you know *it,* the sooner you can work toward *it,* the sooner you can achieve *it,* right? I yearn to have a passion, something that makes me hungry, something that makes me work toward a specific outcome, an *it.* It's the lack of knowing that triggers my fear. The "up-in-the-airness" of no plan is scary.

Which is why, most likely, I am freaked out by the cannabis stock that my grandfather bought for my sister and me a week ago. "I'm telling you," he said at dinner, "this stuff is gonna be big. Just hang onto it for a little while." So, in addition to questioning the legality of the purchase as well as my existence, I spent the past week watching the price of my weed stock on my iPhone app. It kept rising.

"Do you want to sell it?" my grandfather now asks us at dinner this week. I have no idea. I don't know about stocks in general, let alone cannabis stocks. And I don't know about me. Am I striving for millions and going for broke? Or am I playing it safe and cashing in now so that at least I come away with something? My twin sister, of course, knows what she wants to do. She's in it for the long haul.

So is my grandpa. "Let it sit," he advises me. "It'll go up, it'll go down. Just take it day by day. See how it goes, and see how you feel. Eventually a day will come and you'll know what to do with it. It's a gamble, play the game."

I agreed to let it ride. Not that it's easy. Not that I don't check the price of the stock constantly and wonder if I'm doing the right thing. But I'm practicing living with the unknown. I realize now that my grandpa's lesson on pot stock, of all things, is a lesson on life. Life is risky, unpredictable. Even if I, like my sister, knew what kind of game I wanted to play, there's no guarantee of the outcome. Simply having an *it* doesn't guarantee success.

And just because I don't know what my aspiration is, just because I don't have an *it*, doesn't mean I'm not in the game, striving for something. Maybe my *it*, right now, is just to figure out my *it*. Maybe it's good to not have a plan, to let myself exist and see how I feel. Life, like my stock, is a ride, and I just have to be okay with letting my hand play out.

One day I'll know—the answer might even become obvious. But until then, when people ask, "What do you want to do in life?" instead of freaking out and questioning God's purpose for placing me on this Earth, I'll just rephrase the question in my brain: "What do you want to do with your cannabis stock?"

"I'm not sure yet," I'll answer. "I'm taking it day by day."

severe and enduring

Laura Ingram

The hospital windows gnash together like God's overbite, the rain tapping her long fingers against the industrial glass. Sixteen girls and two boys sit cross-ankled on a stained sofa, heads bowed over their books as if in prayer, quiet enough to keep our misery immaculate. I, seventy pounds of gossamer and syncope, knot my legs, thin as embroidery floss, in tattered children's tights, search for my sternum beneath the gray shag sweater my friend outgrew in the third grade. One of the women who watches over the ward, Maria, an English major with a Spanish accent, lines us up by the dining room's double doors for the second snack of the day. She snatches my scapula before I reach the patient refrigerator, pulls my brittle hair back into a braid, several strands slipping through her fingers towards the floor.

"Miss Laura. You know the rules. Don't think staff has forgotten how much peanut butter you can shove under those pretty little fingernails. Sleeves up, hair back, hands on the tabletop," Maria says, toppling me into a chair at table one. I push away the plate of boost pudding and banana slices, appeal to the faint fluorescent lights for the apocalypse of my flickering pulse.

The doctors here worry I will fall and break my hip. I worry my friends will find out I am just stress fractures and semicolons and stop sending me cards covered in curves of cursive. Although on chair rest I'm not allowed to check the mail tray, Maria hands me a pastel paper stack every afternoon. Today there are eight envelopes: my grandmother detailing her Saturday of shelling butterbeans; several sets of haphazard heart sketches from my bespectacled boyfriend; thick packets of Harry Potter fan fiction from my friend Sorena, printed in ten-point Times New Roman to take up as little space on the page as possible.

I read over the wrinkled sheets, curled into the coral couch cushion, small and displaced as a comma splice, tuck the hem of my sweater between my teeth so no one can hear me cry. Someone else cries in the rec room. It's always someone else. The throw pillows are swirled with mascara stains. I don't recognize the pitchy pleas I've plucked from my skull until the echo from the other room ends. I sound like a newborn, pink velour tongue velcroed to teeth, cries from my empty mouth almost inaudible, every hour bringing about the harshest hunger I've ever endured yet live without words for.

Weigh-ins are Monday, Wednesday, and Friday, just like the literature summer camp for high school students I was accepted into three months ago and now can't attend because my parents drove me to Durham two Tuesdays ago, a city gray as cardiac arrest, kept alive by the constant mumblings of machines, plastic clouds dripping down to the injected intersections like a normal saline line.

"It's my body," I said as my parents pulled into patient parking. I didn't try to run, just crossed my arms, ringing my forefinger and thumb around my bicep, fingertips touching, clasped and unclasped the Hello Kitty watch I wear just over my elbow. "I destroy it." They popped the trunk anyway, pulled out swaths of chiffon from the children's department of JCPenney, and ushered me into the foyer with its fake blue fire where a freckled receptionist photographed my faded face for the patient portal system, the computer program where they log all our ugly numbers in pixilated, parallel lines.

We took the elevator upstairs. I watched my mouth not move in the shiny silver surface above the control panel. Dr. Stu, a Yankees fan with chapped cheeks, tipped us toward the armchairs scattered across his cramped office. He sent my parents away with Jennie, my therapist. He steepled his fingers then, elbows on his knees, and told me that, according to my lab work, my liver enzymes were elevated, a harbinger of multiple organ failure in anorexia nervosa, my neck cracking, eyes narrowed.

"You're dying," he said.

My chapped lips cracked and bled around chattering teeth. A half smile. "I know."

Weigh-ins are Monday, Wednesday, and Friday, after we've pissed in a cup and before we've lined up for breakfast. A nurse with stained teeth and spotless scrubs smooths the backs of our green gowns as if she's testing the temperature in a claw-footed tub. She's checking our underwear for coin rolls, half-pound weights, or even the neon magnets provided to each patient for the posting of printed Pinterest quotes and family pictures to the white boards in our Technicolor rooms, each with only one wall painted, doors propped open even as we dress and undress, clasping our dresses and fists, always clenched, crouched, floral fabric covering the air-strike zones dog-eared on our skin, blue and marked as tattered atlas pages. I wait until the child psychiatrist calls my bulimic roommate to swap her pink pills for purple suppositories before I curl into the carpet, seeping across the floor like a coffee spill, do as many crunches as I can before I hear Maria's wooden clogs clacking closer, no—closer, her acrylics clutching the pilling of my pink sweater. "That's enough," she says while I turn away, hollow cheek pressed against the ground, rug burn reddening as I let her roll me over, help me stand. Still, I shake my head.

It's never enough.

Jennie, the therapist with hair the color of Nagasaki's shroom, calls me out of art therapy, pulls the lump she snatched from my throat last session out of her pocket.

"Dr. Stu wants us to send you over to the ER."

My hands, replaced with moths, flutter, light on my throat. I know completely that she means I'll be strapped to a stretcher, that doctors who would never let me use their first names will snap their fingers, ask a nurse for a tray with a tube to thread through my nose and down my throat to feed me, revoke the sole, primal power shared between anorexics, suffragettes, and other wrongly imprisoned protestors—refusal. The roof of my mouth itches and my ears ring. "No," I say, imagining uncooked eggs tossed between gleaming prison bars, Saint Catherine's assertion she could live off the seven sacraments alone.

Jennie wraps a wisp of hair around her right ring finger. "You have the ability to stop him, not me."

I stare at my hands, turn my palms up to watch my pulse waver at the wrist. "I can't—I can't eat. It's like at school, I'd have a juice carton in the cafeteria, one with a little striped straw, or a single spoonful of ice cream straight from the container when I got home because, yeah—I was *hungry.*" The syllables make the wrong shape in my mouth: isosceles. I start to cry. "I was hungry, but it didn't matter! This is just who I am! Some girls have acrylic nails and chipped teeth, others have high ponytails and higher GPAs or spiral notebooks and straight bangs. I have hungry," I think I say, ears ringing, rubbing the fuzzy lanugo hairs on my arm the wrong way. Health class textbooks told me they grow in tufts to keep anorexics warm, but I shiver. I am so sharp. I am so cold.

Jennie uncrosses her ankles, eyes the box of colored Kleenex but doesn't reach for it. Jennie thinks handing someone a tissue is asking them to clean up their mess. My parents think she is too liberal. Jennie has too many bumper stickers, is probably bisexual, and definitely swears a lot. I take two tissues unprompted, put them in my skirt pocket. I always keep things I think are pretty, usually whatever my mother would want to throw away from my school bag.

"Helen Keller could see that you're anorexic, Laura. But, Jesus, I've worked with teenage vanishing acts my entire career, and you aren't just hungry. You have a vocabulary taller than *World Book* and *Britannica* combined. You save pink tissues and patterned paper scraps. Your mind is a mountain range. Your hands are paper cranes. You are starving for information, ravening on your knees for a world where the physics of absence is better understood, where you aren't locked in a freezing hospital ward with a gang of girls who cry over soda crackers, or measuring yourself by how much space is left over after you scoot into the school bus seat." She says, or maybe doesn't say—everything's stopped and static as a tornado watch, and I wilt, bones scattered like a jigsaw puzzle shaken onto a rug before it's pored over and put together.

I know the theory of light and matter, the distance formula, at least three of Edgar Allen Poe's poems, how to say "shit happens" in French and German, but I don't know how to respond to this neurotic, weepy woman, so odd and determined. I spend the rest of our hour drawing wilted flowers in the dollar-store journal she gave me the day I admitted, hair hanging half-mast. She demands nothing else, walks me to my room with her fingers closed around my shoulder, heels clacking as she trots the other way.

I draw the blinds, cover my eyes with my hands, and crawl beneath the quilt my mom made although it's four in the afternoon.

I sleep through supper, chew my charred dreams.

the pearly gates

Megan Meyerson

The Pearly Gates looked less . . . well . . . pearly than I had imagined. Sure, Saint Peter stood before them, there was a distant echo of angels singing, and a faint scent of flowers floated on a warm, gentle breeze. But sitting atop the brilliant gold of the Gates twisted a menacing spiral of barbed wire.

I stepped up to the pedestal as Saint Peter called out my name.

He seemed to sense my confusion. "This is the back entrance. It's for people who . . . might not make it in."

I didn't like the sound of that. I felt like I had been pretty virtuous in my life and earned a spot in eternal paradise. Or maybe I just really didn't want to take a spot in eternal damnation. "So basically, I'm still on the line?"

"Oh no—your place is secured. I merely need to ask you a question, and we don't like causing traffic through the main entrance." Saint Peter reached into his robes and withdrew a golden scroll. He unraveled it and began to read. "On the twenty-forth of August, in the Year of our Lord 2019, Joseph Stephens departed his mortal life by means of an elevator malfunction."

I was a little annoyed at being reminded of the circumstances of my death, which were both less glorious and earlier than I had wished in life, but I kept my mouth shut.

Saint Peter continued, "It has come to our Lord's attention that this was the result of a mishap on the part of Joseph Stephens's Guardian Angel, who was meant, but failed, to protect his charge from the accident." Saint Peter looked up from his scroll into my somewhat baffled eyes. "Before you enter the Kingdom of Heaven, you must decide your Guardian Angel's fate."

I stared at Saint Peter. "You're joking."

He looked surprised. "I assure you, I am not."

I thought it unlikely that a saint in charge of admission to Heaven would lie, so I didn't question him further.

"What are my options?" I asked.

"Whatever you wish. You can banish him to a mortal life, take away his status as a Guardian Angel, or force him into eternal poopy-scooping service in Hell." Saint Peter paused, thinking. "You may also forgive him and grant him total exoneration of his sins. It *has* happened occasionally, that someone has chosen that path. Please, take your time."

He dismissed me with a wave of his (I suppose) holy hand. An old woman stood behind me, so I stepped out of her way to let Saint Peter deal with her admittance.

I sat down on a puff of cloud to consider my choices. I had very little experience in making decisions, but what little I did have told me to make a pros and cons list.

On the one hand, the angel had hurt my family greatly in not saving me. I could only shudder, thinking of the grief they must be suffering even now; I imagined my dad's wretched tears, my mom's shattered smile that would crumble at the news of my death, my wife's life as she would try, and perhaps succeed, perhaps fail, to adjust to a life without me.

And because of this angel, I would never know the joys of fatherhood, the quiet happiness of growing old with the woman I loved, or the simple moments in between that count for just as much. I would miss every Christmas morning of pancakes and carols played too enthusiastically, but still adorably, by my child on the piano. I would miss every Mother's Day and Father's Day, miss Easter picnics, miss . . .

But on the other hand, I did not know for what reason he had missed the moment of my death; perhaps he had been saving another, destined to be more important than me, or perhaps preventing some cataclysmic war that would have killed millions. Who was I to judge? The greatest responsibility with which I had ever been entrusted was my dad's twenty-five-year-old station wagon when I was, myself, twenty-five. I could not imagine holding the fate of a human—thousands of humans, for all I knew—in my hands.

I glanced at Saint Peter, but he was busy shuffling papers and sorting out the business of admission to heaven for the old woman.

I rose from my puff of cloud and approached him. It seemed the woman had gained entry, for she thanked Saint Peter heartily and practically skipped through the gates in a manner that seemed to defy the frailness of her frame.

Saint Peter looked up from his papers as I approached. "What did you decide?"

"Can I talk to him?"

Saint Peter sighed. "It would require much paperwork, and it is rather busy today, so you'll forgive me if I say no."

I glanced around. Now that the old woman had passed through the gates, there was no one to be seen.

"Really?" I asked, trying hard to keep the sarcasm from my voice.

"He is unavailable." I raised my eyebrows. Saint Peter sighed and continued in a more genuine tone, "It isn't allowed; I'm sorry. You have to make this decision entirely on your own."

A memory crept suddenly into my mind, of my grandfather telling me to forgive a second-grade bully. I remembered him wiping my tears and saying, "You can only judge a man after you've seen him lose to the turtle and beat the hare." If that went for Guardian Angels as well, I had no business passing judgment on mine if I knew so little about him.

I put my hands in my pockets and tried to look as casual as possible. "I think I'm going to forgive him. You know, no punishment, just a warning ... a 'don't let it happen again,' that sort of thing?"

Saint Peter shook his head absentmindedly as he continued to sort through his papers. "Off to Hell, I'm afraid."

My stomach dropped. Too many words of outrage tried to force themselves from my mouth at once that I stood mutely, staring in utter shock at the saint. *Off to Hell?*

A half growl, half choke finally escaped my throat, and Saint Peter looked up. His brow furrowed. "Wait. You decided on forgiveness?"

I nodded.

"Then you must forgive me, as well; it has been a long few centuries— I'm far overdue for a vacation. I must have misheard you. If you have chosen forgiveness, then it is with great pleasure that I can open the gates and welcome you into the Kingdom of Heaven."

My heart leapt as the barbed wire dissipated into mist and the gates swung open. The scent of flowers floated more pungently on the breeze and the angel choir sounded a little clearer.

I turned, bemused, back to Saint Peter. "And if I hadn't chosen forgiveness?"

He winced. "You would have gone the other direction, at least for now . . . but you would have gotten whatever revenge on your Guardian Angel you desired. From my view, you made the right choice, though; he's really a lovely chap, your angel."

I bowed awkwardly (I was never taught the proper etiquette to use when speaking to a deceased saint) and walked through the gates. My granddad stood just inside, his arms outstretched. As I ran toward him, he winked, and I knew suddenly who had been my Guardian Angel all along.

the nighthawk

Jenna Kurtzweil

One night I lay in want of sleep,
but fair Adventure, dark and deep,
was resting, waiting, captivating
every thought my mind could keep.

And so I stole across my room,
drawn by the Fates' incessant loom,
for whispers, swift and promising,
were luring me into the gloom.

I balanced on the windowsill,
undaunted by the creeping chill
of night, for brightly overhead
the watchful Moon hung soft and still.

Then swiftly, as if by a prayer,
a Nighthawk, slicing through the air,
appeared to rest abreast my lonely
figure as I waited there.

She peered at me through ebon eyes
that sung of shadows, old and wise,
and as she loosed her beak to speak
I listened raptly, hypnotized.

"O Raven-girl, your time is near!
Why must you wither, crouched in dreary,
pallid light? The ballad of your life
is raging! Fly from here!"

I quickly rose, enraptured by
this dark messiah, knowing I
could never flee my bruised and bloodied land
until I learned to fly.

So I, held captive by her claims,
entranced by she who called my name
so boldly, whispered, "Mold me as you will
and make us both the same."

Within a moment, I was changed
and all my features rearranged,
eclipsed by feathers, weathered claws,
and eyes that saw myself estranged.

At this, although the light was dim,
I saw the Nighthawk, old and grim,
take to the skies; within her cries
I heard her final crooning hymn:

"Behold the waxing Moon, and then
look closely as it starts to wane.
Like ragged Ships and rugged Men,
here and there, then gone again."

And just like that, she disappeared,
elusive as the Sisters, weird
and wild; the night once more was mild
and wretched dark no longer feared.

I soared on borrowed wings that night;
bathed in the strange and spectral light
that washed the world, I twirled and balanced,
wraithlike, on the winds of flight.

I skimmed and sailed the velvet sea
that roiled and tossed and cradled me
between the hats and crooked backs
and shadows strewn about the streets.

But Dawn, the Ever-present, curled
her back, and gilded wings unfurled
to usher in the rush of din
that ripped me from my Netherworld.

I woke, as I am wont to do
When Night concedes her glory to
the crystal-patterned mists of Morning's
journey into swirling blue.

And through my window, fading fast,
my loyal Guard did set at last,
obscured and blurred by wishful clouds
that shimmered like a lake of glass.

A lake with waves much stronger then,
or dreams that fade beyond my ken.
Like ragged Ships and rugged Men,
here and there, then gone again.

a petrified conversation

Anna Lund

The word Love
like a pebble under my tongue
It takes a second of awkward maneuvering to dislodge
and tumbles to your feet
We both stare for a moment
I turn my gaze back to your face
and bear witness to a stone of your own pressing against your cheek
You scoop it out
let it rest on your tongue
Then slowly reveal
my undoing
The word Sorry

the laughing spirit

Faith Esene

The kinks were becoming more rebellious. They no longer obeyed when I slathered them with gel and tried to lay them flat with an old toothbrush. My strands had absorbed as much sun as they could handle. I called Auntie Theresa. She would know exactly what to do.

Because of my strong-willed coils, I found myself parked on the side of the road, heart in throat. I had been listening to my favorite song, thinking about how smooth my mornings would be, now that I wouldn't need to worry about my hair. The blaring of the siren startled me. The red, white, and blue streaks cast their shadow over my car. I pulled over, parked, and waited. The officer tapped on the glass. I rolled down the window and greeted him with a cleverly woven calm.

"Ma'am, can I see your license and registration?"

This needed to be done as quickly and as painlessly as possible. If done well, my chest would still be rising and falling when this was over. I suppose I should not have judged this police officer. Yet, given the time continuum of deaths at the hands of uniformed men, the faces plastered all over the headlines, and "Black Lives Matter" dyeing the fabric of reality, I couldn't resist the urge to use my defense mechanisms. Fear could be buried for a moment, but if probed enough, it would eventually come oozing out. I knew that much. It was best to avoid putting your hand in your pocket, so that you did not evoke suspicion. Suspicion pulled back the curtain. Fear would sneak out of hiding, even if the officers weren't aware it had been hiding in the first place. Fear would pull the trigger.

"Ma'am, can I please see your license and registration?"

I took a deep breath.

"Sir, you can retrieve it."

I aimed at the glove compartment with my lips and held my hands up. As a child, I had learned the art of lip-pointing. If my parents ever wanted you to place something on the table or retrieve an item, you would simply follow the direction of their protruding lips. Not everything needed to be spoken, and you never argued with authority. They taught us well. The tension melted as the officer's smirk said *Don't get smart with me.* He knew exactly what I was getting at.

"Ma'am, that's okay. Open the glove compartment, and get the documents I requested."

"Okay, sir."

I needed to reassure him that this girl with dark melanin, wearing an even darker headscarf and black T-shirt, was not a threat. He had to know exactly what I was doing at every moment.

"Sir, I am lowering my hands; I am opening the glove compartment and retrieving my wallet. I am pulling out my license and registration." I handed him the documents, and he nodded in approval.

"Thank you, ma'am. I just wanted to let you know that your tag sticker is upside down. It is best that you replace it as soon as possible if you aren't able to peel it off and turn it the correct way."

"Okay, I will make sure I get that done."

"Alright, ma'am, have a good one."

As the police officer disappeared behind my rearview mirror, the purring of my car engine broke the awkward silence of trying to collect my thoughts. Now I was late for my appointment. I drove a few miles before I turned up the music again. That afternoon, Auntie Theresa braided my hair so stiffly. I held each braid individually so that my roots were not being pulled too much. I opted out of having a receding hairline by the end of the ordeal. I told Auntie Theresa what happened with the officer, and she laughed.

"Ha ha. Smart move, girl."

She laughed because it was just her way of dealing with these kinds of things. She knew that it had boiled down to life or death. She knew the police officers had a soiled history. Too much black blood slithered on the cold concrete, while their blue uniforms stayed blue. When she touched my shoulder, I felt a spark. I felt it move into me—the laughing spirit. I started laughing too. My braids were too tight, but the laughter rolled out of my mouth, until I began choking on the air bubbles that had sneakily slid into my throat. My head throbbed, but I was glad my hair would be protected for the next couple of months.

That night, as I rubbed my scalp, I wondered who would protect our brothers and cousins and friends. There was no way to know what lurked behind the red, white, and blue shadows. They would have to use their silent weapon. They would have to lip-point.

daisy petals

Caitlin Roberts

My older sister was always a bewildering creature—at least, to me. I was sure that to my mother and father, she was just Delilah, just like I was just Willow. They never blinked when Delilah waltzed around the house, humming tunes from a time before she was born, or when she buried herself beneath wool blankets, so deep that I was surprised she could breathe. I know that I wouldn't have been able to breathe, but then again, Delilah was a different species.

Delilah was older than me by seven years, which might have been part of the reason that we lived in two different worlds. She didn't attend school like I did, which was fine, but it was just another area where our paths diverged. Most days, I never saw her. When Delilah did surface from her room, she wore her hair braided down her back and a yellow sundress, no matter what season it was. I didn't understand how she wasn't cold, but for all I knew, her skin might have been immune to the icy air. From the way everyone treated her, the idea that her skin was made of porcelain was entirely plausible.

The strangest thing about my sister, though, was not her mood swings or the distance she kept from me. It was her favorite activity, which she found time to do even when she was having one of her "rainy days," as mother liked to call them. Delilah liked to pick the petals off daisies and paste them to her skin.

I'd watch her do it when I could. Father always kept a bouquet of daisies on the kitchen table, and whenever they'd disappear from their green, glass vase, I'd start searching. When the sun was warm, I'd find her in the garden. If it rained, she would be in the living room. When the wind blew, it was the front porch. It had taken me a while, but I had memorized each of the spots.

She always had a tin, full of some type of paste, and a bristled paintbrush, which she used to smooth the paste over her skin. Sometimes she put the petals on her arms, often her shins. It was rare, but I once saw her press one of the yellow petals against her cheek.

Delilah would cry while she worked or, if it was a "sunny day," sing one of her songs. Whether there were tears dripping down her cheeks or a grin spread across her face, she was meticulous as she worked. Once she finished, the petals would remain on her skin until they turned from yellow to brown and finally crumbled into dust. Then, Delilah would paste more on. I was fascinated by the whole process; I found it beautiful.

So on an October day, when the sun peeked through the clouds, I pulled the daisies out of their vase and headed out to the garden. I didn't have Delilah's special tin or the paintbrush that she used. They were both hidden in the most forbidden area of the house: her bedroom. But I was determined to wear the petals on my skin, so I held a bottle of Elmer's glue in my grubby, little hand and the daisies in the other.

I knelt on the stone pathway and began to pluck the petals from their stems. I tore the first few, not realizing how gentle I needed to be. Some of the petals blew away in the wind and others slipped between cracks in the stone path, but soon I had a small stack, ready to be used. I slathered my arm in glue and was preparing to lay the first petal down when I heard a scream.

I looked up and saw Delilah standing close by, her yellow dress billowing in the wind. Her skin looked ghostly against the blue sky, and for a moment, I believed she was a figment of my imagination.

"What are you doing?" Delilah cried as she ran and knelt next to me. She yanked the daisies out of my hand, and in my surprise, I didn't protest.

My sister never spoke to me, whether she was happy or sad. It was part of what had made her into such a mystical being, and even now that words had spilled from her mouth, the spell was not broken. I felt as if I should run away and hide rather than remain in the presence of the strange creature that was my sister.

"What are you doing?" Delilah asked again, this time with more force.

"I wanted to put the flowers on," I spoke quietly, refusing to stare into her icy, blue eyes. "Like you do."

"You can't," she insisted. "You can't ever, ever be like me."

"Why not?"

Instead of responding, Delilah looked to the ground and began picking up the scattered daisy petals. Her lips were pressed into a thin line, and I knew that I should leave before she began to cry. But at the age of nine, my curiosity was too much for me to walk away without my questions answered. So if Delilah wouldn't tell me why I couldn't have flower petals, then I wanted to know why she could.

"Why do you always wear the petals?" I asked.

Delilah looked up, seeming almost as surprised as I was that I had the courage to speak again. I found myself staring at the freckles on her nose as she turned my question over in her mind, hopefully forming an answer.

"The things I feel sometimes," she said slowly, as if she were tasting each word carefully on her tongue, "I can't ever explain them in words. It's hard for me to remind myself that I ever felt different. That I can feel different again."

I nodded my head, though none of her words made sense. All I knew was that my sister was talking to me. My sister was talking to *me*, and I wasn't going to stop her.

"When I put the petals on my skin," she continued, "they represent happiness, and when they crumble to nothing, they represent sadness. But the thing is, there are always more petals. There is always more happiness, no matter how many times it turns to dust."

She finished collecting the petals and stood up, walking back toward the path. She didn't say goodbye or invite me to follow her, but I didn't need her to. On that day, the strangest part of her, the obsession with daisy petals, had made her seem more human.

my perspective on racial issues in the u.s.

Audrey Zheng

The contributors to the Blue Marble Review *have always met hard realities with creativity and insight, but 2020 contained a quick succession of particularly devastating occurrences that combined to affect all of us in complex ways. In partnership with Wise Ink Creative Publishing, a publisher that believes that writing can change the world, we put together an essay competition to draw insights from young people as they moved social justice conversations forward. The following essay is from grand prize winner Audrey Zheng, whose personal essay on how cultural ideas of Americanness affect individual responses to racism struck us as a vulnerable criticism of white supremacist institutions and a vibrant call to meet discrimination with our eyes wide open.*

During my fifth-grade colonial fair, the slavery exhibit had the longest line. To learn about the Middle Passage, we curled up in a cardboard box; two boys shook us back and forth until we giggled and tumbled out. The Atlantic slave trade occurred in a time that did not exist to us, so nobody thought of the Black bodies falling to the ocean floor. We had stripped the evil out of history and replaced it with sugary ignorance. We did not know that our thoughtless play was that same evil, rippling across time.

I always assumed that racism only manifested itself in brief moments of malice. Sometimes, my classmates would pull at the edges of their eyelids and speak in a mock Chinese accent. This hurt, but it was rare, an occasional prick. I never thought to look at racism from outside my perspective. I never considered that its effects could be as debilitating as a shard lodged in the flesh.

As a second-generation American with a vaguely Asian accent, I always had the sense that I was foreign to the land I was born in. Nobody assumes that a white person is foreign, regardless of how many generations their family has been in the US. Because this was not a luxury afforded to me, I overcompensated by staunchly defending everything I saw as American. When Colin Kaepernick knelt to the National Anthem, I hurried to voice my offense. Subconsciously, I viewed Americanness as whiteness. By trying to defend America, I was defending white privilege.

One night after George Floyd was killed, my parents and I watched news footage of the mass protests. I didn't realize the extent to which Floyd's death had moved me until my dad commented that "change has to come from both sides." In other words, he thought that Black communities should focus on improving themselves before expecting others to shed their prejudices. I was hit with the heavy realization that ignorance runs through the very veins of this country, igniting bigotry wherever it goes. And I wasn't exempt—I realized that just as racism is present throughout our systems, it was present in me too.

When I heard my dad make that comment, a comment that is far too often repeated by TV anchors or lawmakers, I suddenly felt ashamed. I knew now that racism was not limited to isolated jabs but was systemic. I had been fortunate—in the years since that fifth-grade fair, since I'd first watched Kaepernick take a knee, I'd learned about redlining, the racial motivations behind the War on Drugs, and the eternally exploited loophole in the thirteenth amendment. Without that knowledge, it would have been impossible for me to understand the struggles that Black communities face today. I would have had the exact same view as my dad. Many years ago, in a time that will forever belong to me, I curled up in a cardboard box and laughed as I tumbled about. Soon, my classmates and I will become adults. Some of us will have children of our own. I can only hope that when that time arrives, we will no longer laugh at our own ignorance.

contributor bios

Kate Bishop graduated from the University of Michigan in 2019 and is originally from Leland, MI. Her poetry also appears in *Fortnight Literary Press*, *Blueprint Literary Magazine*, Writer to Writer 2019, and Z Publishing House's *America's Emerging Poets* series.

Sarah Blair is a seventeen-year-old student writer who continues to read, write, and explore poetry. She resides in Troy, NY, where she participates in spoken word slams and open mics.

William Blomerth is currently a bioengineering student at Northeastern University. He hopes to contribute to the improvement of treatments for patients suffering from neurodegenerative and other diseases.

Alexa Bocek is an emerging writer from Pittsburgh, Pennsylvania, whose work has appeared in the *Claremont Review*, *Literary Heist*, *Mystic Blue Review*, *Dime Show Review*, *Blue Marble Review*, and Running Wild Press. She's an editor and staff member of BatCat Press. She was managing editor for *Pulp Literary Magazine* (2018–2019). She's been writing for several years and attends the Roosevelt University of Chicago, studying marketing and writing.

Alexandra Bowman is a freelance illustrator, political cartoonist, and fine artist from Washington, DC. She serves as the editorial political cartoonist for Our Daily Planet, a climate news platform with a readership of 13,000 (which she is told John Kerry reads daily). She was also recently hired as an in-house illustrator for Georgetown University's Office of Communications; her work will be published by Georgetown on all its online and social media platforms to promote the school as well as university events and initiatives. Alex serves as the live political cartoonist for the Georgetown Institute of Politics and Public Service; she creates live illustrations of speakers, having already drawn Bernie Sanders, Pete Buttigieg, Mark Zuckerberg, and others. Alex is also the creator of *The Hilltop Show*, Georgetown University's political comedy show, which seeks to present campus, national, and international news to those who might not otherwise engage with current events. More information about the show can be found at hilltopshow.com. Alex has illustrated three children's books and has had work published by BBC News, BBC Books, Puffin Books, the Georgetown University Institute of Politics and Public Service, and Penguin Random House UK. Her work has been featured by a variety of groups on social media, including Disney XD and *The Late Show with Stephen Colbert*. Alex posts her work on Instagram at @alexandrabowmanart and on Twitter at @scripta_bene.

Anthony DiCarlo is currently pursuing a degree in classical languages and literature from the University of California at Davis. He has had poetry previously published in *RHINO* and *Blue Marble Review* and was the winner of the 2019 Celeste Turner Wright Poetry Prize.

Lilly Dickman is going to be a freshman at the University of Michigan. She is a dancer, a water-skier, a writer, and a twin. Her plays, *What Happens in Springfield* and *Mondays,* were performed in the Short Play Festivals at her high school in 2018 and 2019. She lives in Highland Park, in suburban Chicago, with her parents, her sister, and her dog, Pickles.

Emily Dorffer is an editor who has cerebral palsy. Her poems and short stories have appeared in a variety of markets including *Daily Science Fiction, Cicada,* and *Short Édition.* When she isn't busy writing, she loves baking with her mom and spoiling her cat. You can read more of her works on Wattpad @sandydragon1.

Yuwei Dou is a senior at Amador Valley High School. She is a creative writer, student journalist, page editor, musical theatre actor, and professional Chinese zither player. She is actively involved in school and enjoys joining the community. Yuwei professionally plays the Chinese zither, a 21-string traditional Chinese instrument almost 2,000 years old, which she has done since the age of four; she had already passed Level 10 at 11 years old. She enjoys doing competitions and won first place in the National Chinese Zither Competition from 2009 to 2016. She also writes her own zither pieces including: "Summer"; "That Year, That River"; "Childhood"; "Homeland Grassland, Homeland River"; etc. As a member of the High School Music Collaborative and the leader of PLAY Chinese Ensemble, Yuwei enjoys using music to share the joy and happiness with other people in the community. Yuwei is a creative writer, even though English is her second language and she came to America just three years ago. She has already won the Scholastic Writing Contest, Bay Area Book Festival Writing Competition, and the Tri-Valley High School Writing Competition, as the only double winner. She got the scholarship to study creative writing in CSSSA this summer. She is also the page editor of the Amador Valley journalism class. She always tries her best to make the school and the Pleasanton Unified School District better as a leader in LINK, an active member in Pleasanton SIAC, and a student representative in LCAC and DCLC. She loves musical theatre and did lots of main roles in performances. In her free time, she enjoys listening to music, reading books, and cycling.

Stephen Duncanson studies physics at the University of Connecticut and enjoys long hikes in the woods.

Patrick Erb-White (18) is a poet, playwright, and amateur mathematician. He graduated from Lincoln Park Performing Arts Charter School, where he studied writing and publishing.

Annie Ertle is a copywriter living and working in Cleveland, Ohio.

Faith Esene's previous work has been featured in the *Kalahari Review* and the anthology *Colorism: Essays and Poems*.

Jordan Ferdman is a junior in high school. She is passionate about the usage of the word "girl."

Jaden Goldfain is a sophomore pursing a BA in writing from Point Loma Nazarene University. She has work published in *iō Literary Journal* as well. Jaden has a passion for writing about the things that hide in shadows and for the often-suppressed voice of her generation.

Lucas Grasha is two years out of college and deeply confused about life, as is customary. In those two years, he has gotten married, lived in his second apartment, adopted two cats, and been pretty much adopted by his wife's family.

Noelle Hendrickson is an eighteen-year-old artist based in Washington, DC. She is Adobe licensed and has had art and photography in a number of literary magazines. She is currently studying computer science and art with hopes to become an animation artist in the video game industry.

Shannon Horton is a South African artist based in Saudi Arabia. The medium she uses is mainly watercolor and gouache, but she does love to experiment with multiple mediums like oil paint, pen, and digital art. To help with the creative process, she listens to music and spends time outside with nature. She says there's nothing quite like the feeling of finding a really great song that clicks and resonates deep inside you; that's when she gets most excited to paint. The main subjects she focuses on painting are botanical subjects. Painting is a part of her everyday life, something she can't imagine not doing. It's a passion that's been part of her since the young age of three—creativity has always been encouraged by her friends and family. Shannon tries to pass creative inspiration to others around her, even people who don't believe they're creative themselves.

Chris Howard began making art after raising a family, pursuing a legal career, and becoming a Master Gardener. She creates complex, colorful pen and marker drawings that are inspired by the beauty of the natural world and the colors of her garden as well as current events. The works celebrate the cycle of life: blossoming, beauty, loss, and transformation. These themes are explored through the imagery of butterflies, moths, leaves, birch trees, and flowers. She is currently using her art to explore the experience of having Parkinson's disease.

Laura Ingram is a tiny girl with big glasses and bigger ideas. Her poetry and prose have been published in over seventy literary journals, among them the *Cactus Heart Review, Gravel, Glass Kite Anthology*, and *Voice of Eve*. Her second poetry collection, *Mirabilis*, is forthcoming for 2020 with Kelsay Books. Her first collection, *Junior Citizen's Discount*, was released with Desert Willow Press in May 2018; her children's book *Stand Up* was subsequently released with Nesting Tree Books in August 2018. Laura loves Harry Potter and Harry Styles. She is an undergraduate creative writing student.

Heather Jensen is a senior at Red Mountain High School in Mesa, Arizona. She served as National Student Poet of the Southwest 2018 and is co-president of Creative Youth of Arizona, an organization that administers the Phoenix Youth Poet Laureate program and develops creative opportunities for young Arizonans. Her poetry, short stories, and photography have been published by the Alliance for Young Artists and Writers, Best Teen Writing of Arizona, *Diode Poetry Journal*, *Polyphony HS*, and the Live Poets Society of New Jersey, among others. She is eighteen years old.

Jenna Kurtzweil is twenty-three and hails from Palatine, IL. She wrote "The Nighthawk" as an undergrad at the University of Illinois—now, she lives in Urbana-Champaign and is proudly employed at her alma mater. She is always looking for new opportunities to experience life through travel, literature, music, and all forms of storytelling.

Jessica Lao is a freshman at Harvard who is originally from Atlanta, GA. Her work has been published or is forthcoming in *Rising Phoenix Review*, *New England Review*, *Alexandria Quarterly*, and more, in addition to being recognized by the Alliance for Young Artists & Writers and Live Poets Society. Outside of writing, Jessica has exhibited at the High Museum, Capitol Building, and Savannah College of Art and Design; her art will be exhibited in Paris, Beijing, New York, and Nairobi in the coming year.

Amanda Lee is, above all, Singaporean. Amanda is a student at Raffles Institution, where she is also a member of Writers' Guild. She is a former Creative Arts Programme mentee, and her work has been recognised by the Torrance Legacy Creativity Awards and Teenink Editors' Choice.

Austin Li is a freshman at the University of California, Los Angeles. As a developing artist, he explores various mediums such as painting, installation, and digital media. Studying design/media arts under the arts and architecture department at UCLA, he hopes to further his artistic practices by combining scientific inquiry with artistic exploration. Two of his favorite artists are Salvador Dali, for his wild choice of subject matters, and Claude Monet, for his simple brushstrokes.

Anna Lund is from Bemidji, Minnesota, and currently attending North Dakota State University. She's pursuing majors in visual art and apparel design, works in the NDSU theater department's costume shop, is a board member of PLACE Arts Community and To Be Determined Comedy, and makes time to write on the weekends.

Avra Margariti is a queer social work undergrad from Greece. She enjoys storytelling in all its forms and writes about diverse identities and experiences. Her work has appeared or is forthcoming in *Flash Fiction Online*, *The Forge Literary*, *SmokeLong Quarterly*, the *Journal of Compressed Creative Arts*, *Argot Magazine*, and other venues. Avra won the 2019 Bacopa Literary Review prize for fiction. You can find her on Twitter @avramargariti.

Daniel Marquez is a US marine currently stationed in Parris Island, South Carolina. He is taking media arts and animation college classes online in his free time and continues to pursue his knack for creative expression through writing, journaling, and art. White Bear Lake, Minnesota, is where he calls home.

Megan Meyerson is soon to be a freshman at Columbia, having graduated from Greenwich Academy. She has been published in *Surge* ("A Flower's Dream"), *CT Young Writer's Magazine* ("A Disturbing Neighbor"), and *Daedalus* ("A Look Beyond," "The Devil's Appointment," and "Vader Takes a Taxi"). She was a finalist for Bluefire's $1,000 for 1,000 Words Contest and has won one National and twenty-seven Regional awards from the Scholastic Arts and Writing Awards. She was also the winner of the NEATE Fiction Contest 2019 ("The PB&J Showdown"). She is most inspired by J.K. Rowling, Jane Austen, Charlotte Brönte, Gail Carson Levine, J.R.R. Tolkien, and Brandon Sanderson. She enjoys baking, playing squash for Columbia, and playing with her two dogs.

For as long as she can remember, **Sylvia Nica** has loved literature. She is the co-editor of her school literary magazine and attended the 2019 Kenyon Review Young Writers Workshop. She plans to major in English and pursue a career as a novelist.

Caleb Pan is a stressed-out teenager who enjoys hash browns and crying over his lost 4.0 GPA after (barely) surviving Calculus 1, 2, and 3 along with Differential Equations. He's an avid reader, writer, coder, and martial artist in his free time.

Sophie Panzer is the author of the chapbooks *Bone Church* (dancing girl press 2020), *Mothers of the Apocalypse* (Ethel Press 2019), and *Survive July* (Red Bird Chapbooks 2019). Her recent work has appeared in *Sad Girl Review*, *Coffin Bell* journal, *The Hellebore*, and *Shooter Literary Magazine*. She lives in Philadelphia.

Anishi Patel is a senior at Saratoga High School with a passion for creative writing. Her work has been recognized by the Scholastic Art and Writing awards and is in or forthcoming in *Skipping Stones* magazine, *Blue Marble Review*, and *805 Lit*, among others. Anishi is an editor-in-chief for the *Saratoga Falcon*, and she is also an editor for her school's literary magazine, *Soundings*, and for the *Siblíní Journal*.

Caitlin Roberts is a young author living in Anchorage, Alaska. She has been published in *Blue Marble Review*, *Canvas Literary Journal*, and *Skipping*

Stones literary magazine. When she's not writing, Caitlin can be found performing and choreographing dance routines or simply lazing about with her wonderful dog, Tess. In the coming fall she hopes to attend college for both dance and creative writing.

Deon Robinson is an Afro-Latino poet born and raised in the Bronx, New York. He is an undergraduate at Susquehanna University, where he is the two-time recipient of the Janet C. Weis Prize for Literary Excellence. His work has appeared in *Homology Lit*, *Honey & Lime*, *Kissing Dynamite*, *Occulum* journal, *Okay Donkey*, and the *Shade Journal*, among others. His work was also nominated for the Best of the Net Anthology in 2019. He is pursuing a BA from Susquehanna University, where he hopes to be able to get into an MFA or land himself a fellowship.

Linzy Rosen is studying environmental studies and psychology at Brandeis University. She is passionate about leading menstrual advocacy and environmental sustainability initiatives on campus. Linzy currently writes opinion pieces, covering topics such as politics and misogyny, and has been published in *Teen Vogue*.

Marriya Schwarz is from Northern Virginia and is a recent graduate of the College of William & Mary, graduating with honors and a bachelor's degree in American studies and creative writing. Her writing has been featured in Writopia Lab's From Your Friendly Neighborhood Feminist, *Women's eNews*, and student publications like William & Mary Television's *Ramble On*, *DoG Street Journal*, and *Winged Nation*. When Marriya is not writing, she manages an old haunted building, teaches tap dance classes, and works as a web series producer.

Claire Shang is a New York high school senior. She is a graduate of the

Kenyon Review Young Writers Workshop with work recognized by the UK's Poetry Society, the Scholastic Art and Writing Awards, and Smith College. Besides writing, she also runs and plays the piano, but not all at the same time (yet).

Devika Sharma is a nineteen-year-old sophomore at the University of Texas at Austin. Art is not her major, although she wishes it could be, but she still draws on a regular basis outside of school. She primarily uses pencil and ink to draw people but is hoping to be able to paint someday. She likes to capture interactions between people in her drawings.

Danielle Sherman is seventeen and a junior in high school. She is an executive editor for *Polyphony Lit* and a National Silver Key recipient of the Scholastic Art and Writing Awards. She enjoys painting, reading, and playing soccer and hopes to become an author and editor.

Malcolm Slutzky is a queer trans man and college student from New Jersey. In his free time, he enjoys studying physics and playing Scrabble against himself.

Jayla Stokesberry is a nineteen-year-old college student at UCLA. She is currently studying cognitive science with a minor in Spanish. Besides writing, Jayla enjoys listening to music, taking long walks, big roller coasters, and the beach.

Ellora Sutton, twenty-three, lives in Hampshire, England, where she is currently studying toward a master's in creative writing. Her work has been published by *The Cardiff Review*, *Mookychick*, *Poetry News*, and *Poetry Birmingham Literary Journal*, amongst others. She won first place in the 2019 Pre-Raphaelite Society poetry completion and the 2019 Hampshire Prize, part of the Winchester Poetry Prize. Her debut chapbook will be published by Nightingale & Sparrow in September 2020. You can find her on Twitter @ ellora_sutton.

Henry Wahlenmayer is a freshman at Oberlin College. His plays have been performed at Lincoln Park Performing Arts Center and Pittsburgh City Theater, and he is a 2019 Young Playwrights Festival winner. From 2017 to 2019 he was the writer and director of the Ensemble Immersion Theater Company, and his short fiction has appeared in *Pulp* magazine. He'd like to thank everyone at *Blue Marble* for their continued support and also Colleen Ballinger and Tara Draper for all their help with this story.

Velda Wang is a rising senior at Parkview High School in Atlanta. She creates art as a form of self-expression of what cannot be expressed in words and as a bridge between herself and society. In her free time, she enjoys teaching underserved children art through her nonprofit organization, Young Artists Atlanta, because she realizes the impact art has had on her and hopes to foster that in others.

Sierra Woelfel is a writer from Kansas City, Missouri. She attended Lincoln Park Performing Arts Charter School before the University of Central Missouri to get her bachelor's in communications. In her spare time, she studies theology, politics, and textiles.

Arden Yum is a junior at Trinity School in New York City. Her favorite subjects are Latin, English, and math. She enjoys photography, teaching, and oatmeal. Her work has been recognized by the Scholastic Art and Writing awards.

Audrey Zheng is sixteen years old and a junior in high school.

about blue marble review

Blue Marble Review is a Minneapolis-based nonprofit online literary journal that publishes the work of student writers and artists ages 13–22. Submissions are accepted via our website, www.bluemarblereview.com, and evaluated by a rotating panel of both teen and adult editors. Although we are based in the United States, our writers and artists send work from all over the globe. Issues are published quarterly in March, June, September, and December—along with short poetry-only "supplements" that appear online in January and July.

Blue Marble Review accepts poetry, personal essays, fiction, short stories, and travel writing as well as hybrid forms and the occasional research paper. We also welcome photography and art submissions, with guidelines for submitting found on our website. Submissions are accepted on a rolling basis and open all year long. Each issue is available free online and later archived on our site. This is our first anthology.

Our mission from the beginning has been to encourage young writers and artists and to emphasize that creative work and stories do matter. The goal of our journal is to assemble in each issue a broad range of voices, perspectives, and life experiences.

support blue marble review

Blue Marble Review is a nonprofit organization and completely dependent on grant funding and donations from contributors who believe in the power of literacy and young writers. We invite you to join us in supporting our talented contributors as well as our student editors, as they become our future teachers, writers, creators, and leaders.

Donations of any amount can be made via the link on our site at: bluemarblereview.com/donate/

acknowledgments

Blue Marble Review began five years ago with a mission to engage and encourage young writers, and we've had plenty of help along the way.

We're grateful to Amy Masson and SUMY Designs, who got us up and running and continues to maintain and provide stellar technological support for our website.

Talented and creative Mary Kay Warner of Sandhill Studio listened to our vision, helped us distill our mission, and then created a beautiful logo for all our issues and correspondence.

Our journal was always meant to be a place where art and writing came together, and we were lucky from the very beginning, when the universe aligned us with Minneapolis artist Chris Howard, whose work graced our very first issue and served as outstanding cover art throughout our first year of publication.

Sincere thanks to Susan Solomon, editor extraordinaire of *Sleet Magazine* for shared wisdom, astute advice, and generous encouragement in the early days of *Blue Marble Review*. Additional thanks to Pamela Schmid, creative nonfiction editor of *Sleet,* who willingly shared her expertise on reviewing and editing submitted work.

Much gratitude to our anonymous donors and grant givers, who fly under the radar but give with an enthusiasm that enables us to continue to pay our editors and our contributors and keep our website thriving.

A huge thanks to director Krista Hitchcock and the students at the Minnetonka High School Writing Center in Minnetonka, Minnesota, who welcomed us in the early days of *Blue Marble* and in the early morning hours—with a ready-to-go roundtable of editors, and an eagerness to read and review submitted work.

Our sincere thanks to current and former Tonka Writers Meili Gong, Isabella Milacnik, Alexa Vos, Priscilla Trinh, Katie Ward, Kate Schiltz, Becca Schumacher, Faith Quist, Anne Malloy, Maya Schroff, Ellie Retzlaff, Addie Gill, and others who added reading, reviewing, and editing for our journal to their already-packed high school schedules.

Thank you to Victoria Petelin, Patrick Maloney, and the team at Wise Ink Creative Publishing for guidance and leadership in taking this project from concept to completion. This anthology simply wouldn't exist without your expertise.

We're inspired and grateful to have worked with talented designer Jack Walgamuth, who understood our aesthetic and our mission, and then created an incredible cover and book design for our first anthology.

To computer whiz Chris Hill, never more than an emergency text away, endless thanks for ongoing tech support, great advice, and good humor.

And most importantly to the student writers and artists who found us from all over the world—kudos to all of you for your creative courage and for generously allowing us to feature your work in our past issues and in this anthology.